Peterson Field Guide Coloring Books

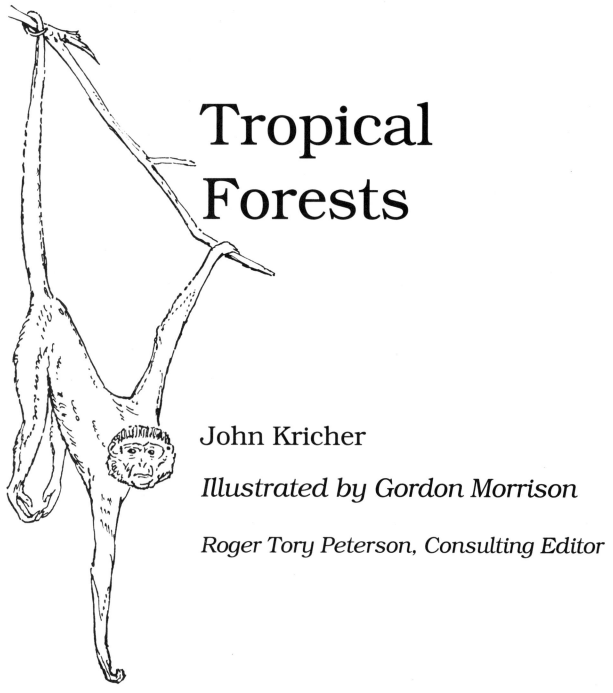

# Tropical Forests

John Kricher

*Illustrated by Gordon Morrison*

*Roger Tory Peterson, Consulting Editor*

*Sponsored by
the National Wildlife Federation
and the National Audubon Society*

Houghton Mifflin Company  Boston  New York

For information about permission to
reproduce selections from this book,
write to Permissions, Houghton Mifflin
Company, 215 Park Avenue South,
New York, New York 10003.

Printed in the United States of America

DPI  17  16  15  14  13  12  11 10 9 8

# Introduction

Exploring the outdoors requires a quick eye, one that is trained to see details. The color of a bird's wing, the shape of a tree's leaves, or the pattern of a butterfly's spots are details that distinguish these species from other similar ones. To help them identify plants and animals, most beginning naturalists soon learn to use Field Guides, such as the *Field Guide to Birds.* These handy, pocket-size books offer short cuts to identification, with clear illustrations complete with arrows pointing to the special features of each species.

This coloring book is a field guide for those who want to sharpen their powers of observation. By filling in the illustrations during evenings at home, you will condition your memory for the days you spend outdoors identifying animals and plants. You will learn to recognize the vast variety in the subtle colors of the forest. And you will read about why many of the animals in this book are in danger of becoming extinct.

Exploring the outdoors, watching the birds and other animals, can be many things — an art, a science, a game, or a sport — but it always sharpens the senses, especially the eye. If you draw or paint, you transfer the images of your eye and mind onto paper. In the process, you become more aware of the natural world — the real world — and inevitably you become an environmentalist.

Because most of our tropical rain forests are in distant parts of the world — and disappearing fast — most of us will never get the chance to see a Jaguar or a Scarlet Macaw in its native habitat. But as environmentalists, we still care deeply about these and all the planet's species, and work to preserve them.

Most of you will find colored pencils best suited for coloring this book, but if you are handy with brushes and paints, you may prefer to fill in the outlines with watercolors. Crayons, too, can be used. Don't labor too much over getting the colors just right; have fun, but remember the plight of the tropical plants and animals you are getting to know.

Roger Tory Peterson

# About This Book

Around the equator lie the tropics, a hot, wet part of the Earth where living things flourish. Much of the tropics is covered with rain forests (often called "jungle") that are the most spectacular habitats on our planet. Their tall trees are home to an awesome variety of plants, birds, monkeys, insects, and other animals — so many, in fact, that most biologists agree that fully half of the world's species live in rain forests and other tropical habitats. Yet rain forests cover, at most, 10% of the world's land.

If you take a walk through about two acres of temperate forest, such as those in New England, Wisconsin, or West Virginia, you will encounter about two dozen species of trees. On a stroll through two acres of South American rain forest, however, you might pass 250 to 500 kinds of trees. You might also find between 100 and 200 bird species, over 50 mammal species, and a staggering 42,000 different kinds of insects! You might find growing on a single rain forest tree up to 50 species of vines, air plants, cacti, orchids, and other plants. The South American country of Colombia has 1,695 bird species, over twice as many as all of North America.

This coloring book is our attempt to introduce you to the almost innumerable wonders of the world's rain forests. Although rain forests occur on many continents, nowhere are they more remarkable than in Central America and in South America, in the area around the great Amazon River. The climate is right for rain forests and cloud forests in most of South America and in all of the Central American countries, as far north as the southeastern corner of Mexico. Rain forests

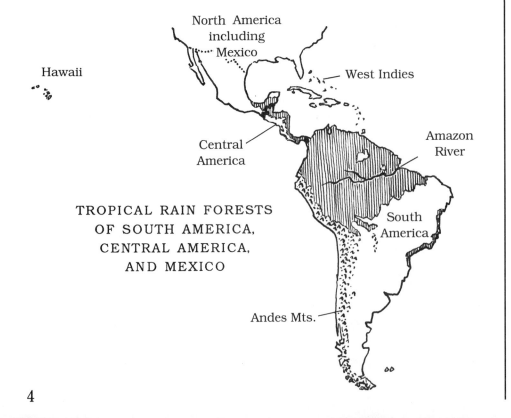

TROPICAL RAIN FORESTS
OF SOUTH AMERICA,
CENTRAL AMERICA,
AND MEXICO

are found in the lowlands, and cloud forests (named for the cool cloudlike mist that usually hangs in the air) cover tropical mountainsides. Tropical American forests are the major focus of this coloring book. However, we have included a quick look at the remarkable creatures found in the rain forests of Africa, Asia, and Australia. (Note: In this book, the word *American* refers not to the United States of America but to the land mass that includes all the Americas — North, South, and Central.)

## A Walk Through a Rain Forest

What is a tropical rain forest like? Suppose you could suddenly be transported to Brazil, where the immense Amazon River meets the mighty Negro River, and stand beneath the towering trees of the Amazonian rain forest. The first thing you notice is the hot, sticky air. The air temperature is around 90°F and the humidity near 100%. You begin to sweat, even standing still. You might feel as though you are breathing water. You look up at the sky, watching as the scattered puffy clouds give way to thicker and darker rain clouds. You feel the first drops and hear the sound of rain hitting the thick, waxy leaves that clothe the immense trees surrounding you. Suddenly the heavens seem to open up and you are caught in a real tropical cloudburst. Rain falls so fast you can barely see ahead of you. The dense trees afford some shelter, but still you are soaked. The deluge may last only a few minutes or most of the day.

Expect to get wet when you visit a tropical rain forest. They are very well named — most tropical rain forests receive at least 80 inches of rain in a year (at least twice as much as most places in North America). Some rain forests receive between 200 and 300 inches of rain each year!

Warm and wet are the two key words that describe the climate of a tropical rain forest. The temperature rarely drops below 80°F, so of course it never snows and there is no cold winter. However, most tropical areas do have seasons. There is typically a "rainy season," when rain falls continually, and a "dry season," when skies are mostly clear.

Life thrives where there is plenty of water plus warm temperatures. This is perhaps the most important reason why the world's tropics have so many different kinds of plants and animals. Plants ranging from simple algae and lichens to complex trees, vines, and orchids all succeed in tropical climates. Animals, both those with backbones like birds, mammals, reptiles, and amphibians, and those without backbones, like insects, scorpions, spiders, centipedes, and even flatworms all flourish in the hot, moist tropics.

A first look at a tropical rain forest can be a trifle intimidating. The trees are so tall that even with binoculars, it's difficult to see birds and monkeys in the treetops. The forest floor seems dark no matter what the weather, because almost all of the light is absorbed by the tall canopy, often at least 100 feet from the ground. Strange sounds of unfamiliar birds and insects pierce the silence. In a forest gap, a huge tree has fallen and taken several others with it, creating an opening where light floods in and animals are very active.

Even though there are more kinds of animals in a tropical rain forest than in any other kind of habitat, they are quite secretive and very well hidden. The challenge of spotting them requires luck plus observational skill. Look closely at the tree bark — there could be several kinds of insects sitting in plain sight, but so elegantly camouflaged that they are easily overlooked. Walk the trail in utter silence. You may pass a herd of peccaries, a little Agouti, or even a mighty Jaguar, but if these creatures hear you first, you'll never see them.

Scan the treetops high overhead. Many kinds of tropical trees bear nutritious fruits, eagerly sought by mammals and birds. A fruiting tree is an ideal spot to see parrots and monkeys. Many kinds of tropical birds travel together as they seek out food. One moment the forest may seem birdless, then suddenly you may be surrounded by a flock of 40 or more species — antbirds, tanagers, and many others — so many that you don't have time to see them all.

The more you study rain forests, the more you will be astonished by what they reveal about life on Earth. Take this book with you to zoos, botanical gardens, and natural history museums that display tropical plants and animals.

Better yet, visit a rain forest. Airplanes and cruise ships make it possible for the whole family to take a tropical vacation. Puerto Rico, Jamaica, and Costa Rica all have magnificent tropical rain forest and are within easy reach. Ecuador, Venezuela, and Brazil are farther away, but still just an airplane ride from Miami. There is even some tropical rain forest in the United States, on the Hawaiian Islands, and many kinds of tropical plants and animals can be found in South Florida.

## How To Use This Book

This coloring book will introduce you to over 200 species of rain forest plants and animals. This may seem like a lot, but it is merely a tiny sample of the total. Read the descriptions; at the end of each one is a number that matches one of the small color illustrations at the front and back of the book. These illustrations show you the plant or animal's real colors. Crayons or colored pencils work best to color the pictures.

You'll be surprised how easily you develop an eye for detail. Seeing detail — a distinctive stripe, a characteristic pose — is a key to becoming a skilled naturalist. You may only glimpse a monkey high in a treetop, or see a parrot flock for a few seconds as they flash overhead. Knowing how to recognize key field marks, those few unique characteristics that identify the creature, can spell the difference between frustration and enjoyment.

## The Disappearing Tropical Forests

Unfortunately, the great rain forests of the planet are being cut down at an alarming rate. This is called *deforestation,* and it happens every day of every year. Forests are removed for lumber or to make room for cattle ranching, farming, tree plantations, or mining. In the time it has taken you to read from the beginning of this book, about 150–200 acres of tropical rain forest has been cut.

Over half of the world's tropical rain forests are already gone, and the remaining forests are disappearing at an average of 25–50 acres per minute. The largest tract of rain forest left is the vast Amazon Basin, in South America. African, Asian, and Australian rain forests have largely disappeared. In the Old World, only New Guinea still has most of its native forests intact.

Loss of so much rain forest is tragic for many reasons. One very practical reason is that rain forests supply many of our needs. Woods such as bamboo, mahogany, rosewood, and rattan come from the tropics. Many important foods are tropical in origin: bananas, mangos, papaya, potato, tomato, yams, coffee, cashew nuts, sugar, chocolate, corn, and rice, to name but a few. Spices such as chili pepper, nutmeg, and ginger are from tropical plants. Many things we take for granted, from chewing gum to rubber tires, are from the tropics. For us to continue using these products, as well as to discover new ones, we need to preserve rain forests.

Thousands of rain forest plants have medicinal uses. For instance, the powerful drug curare, a muscle relaxant, is from a tropical plant. Tropical plants may hold the keys to treatment of many medical problems, but if the forests all are cut, this knowledge will be lost forever.

The unrivaled plant and animal diversity of tropical rain forests is, in itself, worth our efforts to conserve. Rain forests can teach us much about life on Earth, about how evolution works in shaping the interactions among life forms. The tropics are a treasure in natural art forms — a great gallery of diversity, a great library of knowledge, a great symphony of sounds. Tropical rain forests are too valuable to lose.

John Kricher

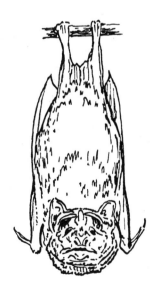

1. A tropical tree

## Tropical Trees, Flowers, and Vines

You see before you a **typical tropical tree (1),** ready for coloring. Tropical trees tend to be slender and tall. The tallest, like the one shown here, grow to heights of 150 feet or more. They tower above the rest of the trees, which are usually about 80 to 100 feet tall.

Tropical trees have lollipop-shaped crowns when they are small. As they grow taller, though, their branches stay clustered near the top of the tree, and the trees take on the shape of an umbrella. Most kinds of tropical trees have straight trunks, and their bark is often smooth and somewhat thin. The tree base is usually supported by roots that extend out over the ground.

High in the treetops, or *canopy,* you will find many other kinds of plants living on the tree's branches or entwining around them. Numerous air plants, such as this **bromeliad (2),** grow on the surface of tree branches. *Vines* of many species hang from the tree or wrap around it.

Because the climate is hot and generally wet throughout the entire year, most tropical rain forest trees are evergreen, meaning they keep their leaves all year long. No snow ever falls on a tropical rain forest! In some places, however, the dry season is so dry that many tree species drop their leaves until the rainy season begins again.

There are many different species, or kinds, of trees in the world's tropics, though many tend to look quite alike and it can be difficult to tell them apart. In Costa Rica, just over 200 tree species have been identified in just 120 square yards of forest, an area about the size of a large swimming pool. In Peru, one researcher found nearly 300 tree species growing on just over one acre.

A close look at a typical tropical tree reveals some of the adaptations that help the tree survive in the hot, wet rain forest. Most trees have **buttressed roots (3)**, which flare out from the trunk as high as 10 feet above ground. Buttresses probably help support the tree, as most tropical soils are so dense and poor that roots do not penetrate deeply. (In buildings, a buttress is a structure that is built against a wall to support it.) Buttresses also enable the roots to easily spread over the ground surface, where they can find the minerals the tree needs (see pages 14–15).

Leaves of tropical rain forest trees are usually smooth along the edges, not lobed, notched, or pointed like the leaves of northern oaks and maples. Tropical leaves are thick and waxy, which helps protect the leaf from invasion by fungi and bacteria and holds in nutrients that could wash away in heavy downpours. Leaves also have **"drip tips" (4)** to shed water.

**Orchids** are among the most common *epiphytes*, or air plants. They anchor themselves in the mosses, lichens, and soil that accumulate on tree branches, and get their water from the air. Many orchids store water in their bulblike bases. Orchids have among the most beautiful of flowers, which can be almost any color. They are pollinated by various insects, especially bees. **(5)**

**Philodendrons** are common house plants in North America. They grow wild in the tropics, many as vines attached to tree trunks. These plants are easily recognized by their large, often heart-shaped leaves. **(6)**

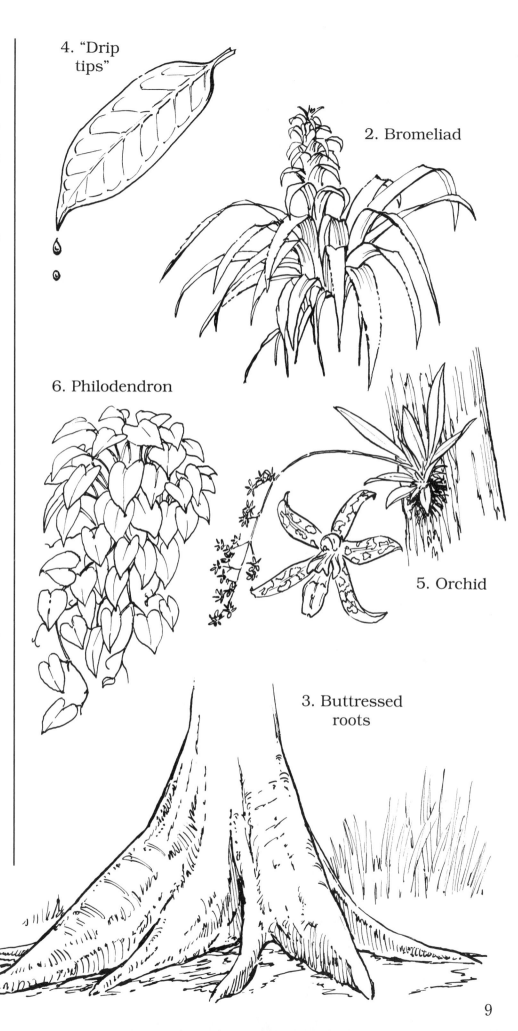

4. "Drip tips"

2. Bromeliad

6. Philodendron

5. Orchid

3. Buttressed roots

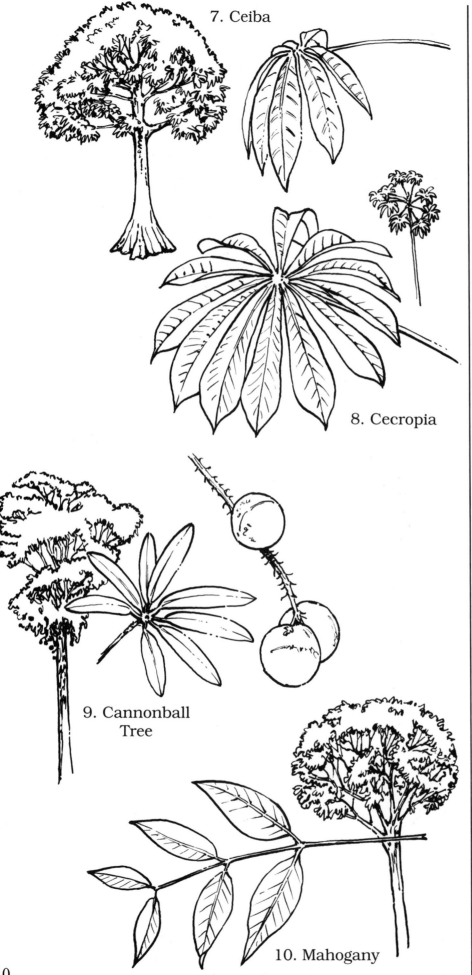

7. Ceiba

8. Cecropia

9. Cannonball Tree

10. Mahogany

The **Ceiba,** or Silk-Cotton Tree, is one of the most majestic of all tropical tree species. Also called the Kapok tree, this giant often reaches heights of over 100 feet. Ceiba leaves are dark green, with from 5 to 8 leaflets hanging from a common stalk. The tree produces large white flowers, which bloom at night and are pollinated by bats. Seeds are surrounded by a feathery material, the "silk cotton" that gives the tree its common name. The silk cotton helps the wind disperse the seeds. We use the material in pillows, mattresses, and life preservers. **(7)**

Smaller than Ceibas, but just as distinct in appearance, **Cecropia** trees line tropical roadsides and grow in open, sunlit areas. Cecropias have spindly trunks like bamboo, very light in color. The leaves look like huge umbrellas. Cecropias grow rapidly, especially in disturbed areas. Many kinds of birds, insects, bats, and monkeys feed on the long fingerlike flowers and fruits. **(8)**

The unmistakable **Cannonball Tree** is closely related to the Brazil Nut Tree. Its large, pale red flowers grow directly from the tree trunk. These flowers, which bloom mostly at night, mature into robust rounded fruits, the "cannonballs." The ripe fruits have a foul odor. **(9)**

The **Mahogany** tree is one of the most important lumber trees of the American tropics. Its reddish brown wood is very hard and beautiful, ideal to use in building furniture, houses, and ships. Mahogany is native to Central America and northern South America. A typical tree grows to about 100 feet tall. Regrettably, because they are so valuable, Mahogany Trees have been completely removed from many areas. **(10)**

*Many tropical trees are planted as ornamentals because they have beautiful blossoms. Here are some of the most common of this colorful group.*

The **Frangipani** has many thin trunks and bright reddish orange flowers. Leaves are large and oblong. Frangipanis are native to the West Indies and Central America. Because it is a small tree (only about 15 feet tall) with multiple trunks, a flowering Frangipani resembles a large bouquet. One variety has white flowers. **(11)**

The **Poinciana** or Flamboyant Tree is widely planted throughout the West Indies, especially on the island of Puerto Rico. Also known as the Flame Tree, it has bright orange, scarlet, or red flowers. The tree grows to 50 feet tall and, like so many tropical trees, has a wide-spreading crown. It is a native of the island of Madagascar (page 58). **(12)**

The unmistakable **Yellow Poui,** or Gold Tree, is native to northern South America and Central America and also occurs on Trinidad and Barbados in the West Indies. The tree has large trumpet-shaped yellow blossoms that cover the tree during the early part of the dry season, when the tree is leafless. The wood is extremely hard and termite resistant. **(13)**

The **Cordia** or Geiger Tree is a native of the American tropics that has been planted throughout the West Indies, Bermuda, the Bahamas, and tropical Mexico. It has clusters of delicate orange-red flowers. Unlike many tropical trees, the Cordia needs little water and does well in dry areas near the coast. **(14)**

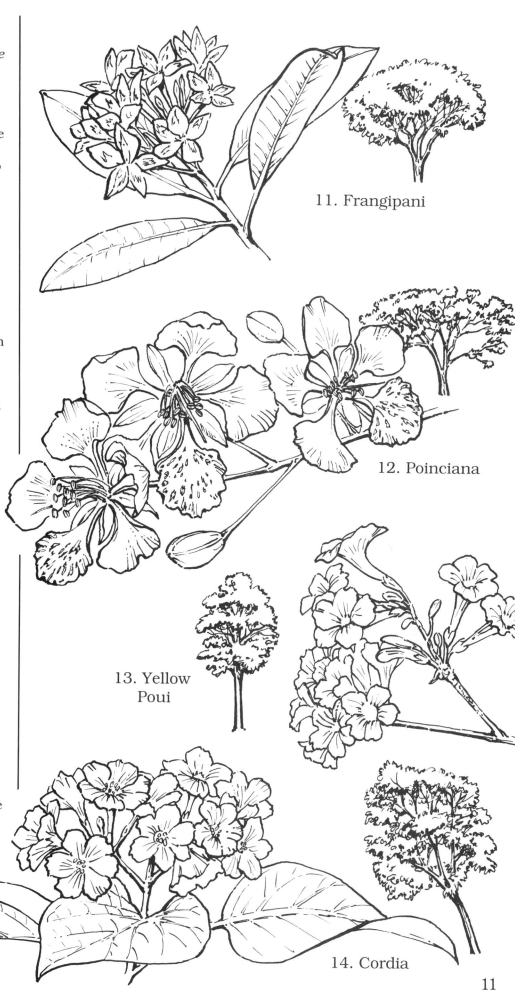

11. Frangipani

12. Poinciana

13. Yellow Poui

14. Cordia

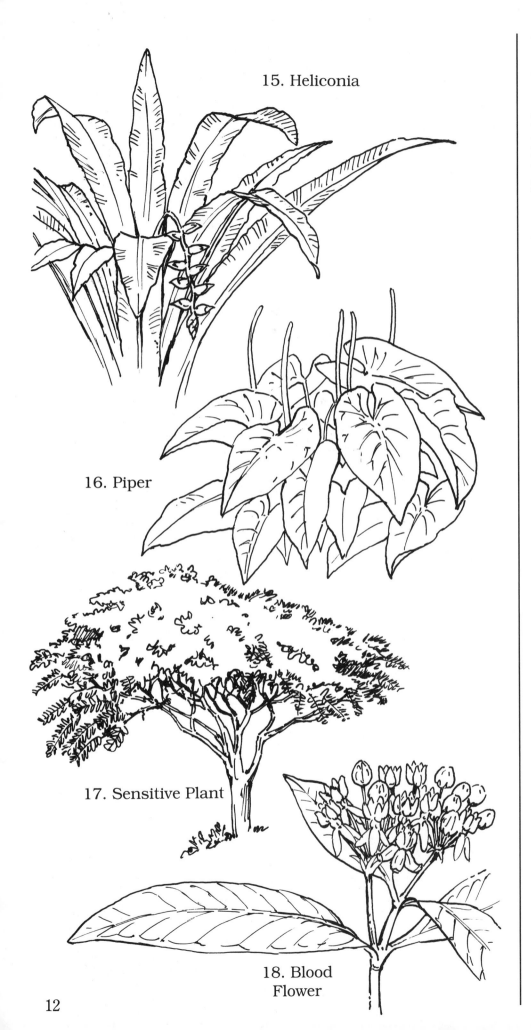

### 15. Heliconia

### 16. Piper

### 17. Sensitive Plant

### 18. Blood Flower

*Tropical roadsides and fields are the habitats for some very colorful and interesting tropical shrubs and wildflowers.*

Perhaps the most obvious plant of tropical roadsides is the **Heliconia,** with its long, immense leaves and bright red, yellow, or orange blossoms. The name Heliconia means "sun-loving," and these plants tend to grow best in sunlit areas such as forest openings, fields, and roadsides. The actual flowers are quite small, located within large, colorful, and sharply pointed bracts that hang from the branches. Heliconias are pollinated by hummingbirds (page 33). **(15)**

The odd **Piper** is a shrub recognized by its curious, pencil-shaped white flower stalks, which give the plant its Spanish name, *candelillo*, or candle-plant. The leaves are large and heart-shaped. Piper flowers are visited by many kinds of bees, flies, and beetles, which help cross-pollinate the plants. Bats eat the Piper fruits and spread the seeds. **(16)**

The **Sensitive Plant** or Mimosa has delicate, feathery leaves and rounded pink flowers. Sensitive Plants are so-named because when their leaves are touched, they fold and droop, seeming to instantly wilt. Mimosas are members of a huge family of plants called legumes, which are known for their ability to take nitrogen from the air and add it to soil to make food. **(17)**

The colorful orange-red **Blood Flower** or Red Head is a common member of the large Milkweed family. Flowers grow in clusters of 5-petaled yellow flowers surrounded by 5 orange outer petals. The seeds grow in pods, and are blown by the wind on their feathery little "parachutes." There are about 150 Blood Flower species. **(18)**

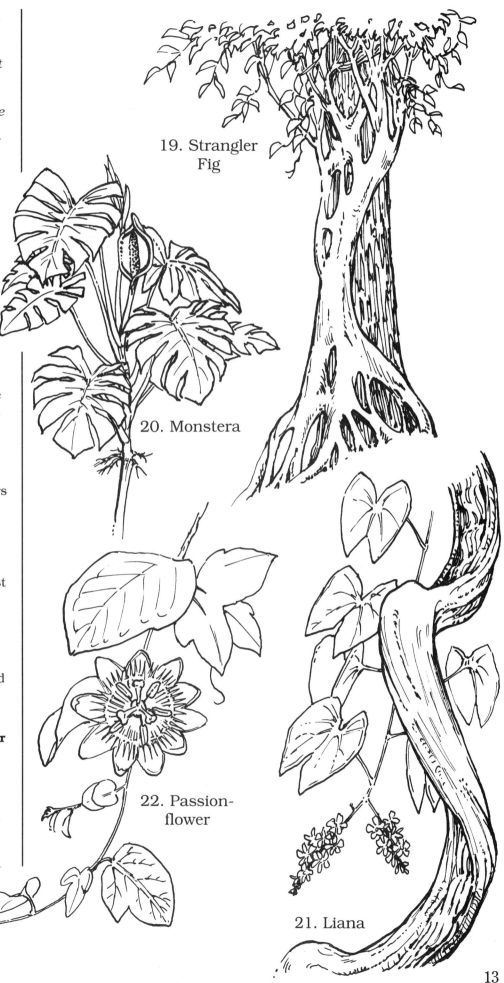

*The vision of Tarzan swinging on a vine through the dense African rain forest is part of our jungle lore. Vines, indeed, are abundant in all rain forests. They grow up and around tree trunks or hang like ropes loosely draped from the high canopy. Many kinds grow best in open areas with plenty of sunlight.*

One of the most notorious tropical vines is the **Strangler Fig.** The vines encircle a tree trunk, growing together until they become so dense that the host tree cannot grow or get enough sunlight. The host often dies, leaving the Strangler in its stead. Stranglers are "planted" by birds, who feed on the figs and drop the seeds on tree branches. **(19)**

The **Monstera,** or "Swiss Cheese Plant," is related to the northern Jack-in-the-Pulpit. This large-leaved vine begins life on the forest floor, growing toward the nearest tree, then up its trunk. Monstera has large, white flowers and is often kept as a house plant. **(20)**

**Lianas** are coiled, spiraling, ropelike vines that hang down from the treetops. They grow first as shrubs on the shady forest floor, but send out runners that grow up into the tall canopy. A single liana may intertwine among several huge trees. Some Amazonian lianas are hollow and contain drinkable fresh water. **(21)**

The large, colorful **Passionflower** is also a vine, but one that prefers areas high in sunlight, such as the forest edge or a gap created by the fall of a tree. Passionflower leaves contain the poison cyanide, which helps protect them from insects, but caterpillars of Heliconius butterflies (page 40) eat them with no difficulty. **(22)**

19. Strangler Fig

20. Monstera

22. Passion-flower

21. Liana

rain

carbon
dioxide

oxygen

water

sunlight

## Recycling in the Rain Forest

Trees constantly recycle water and oxygen. They take in carbon dioxide ($CO_2$) from the air and water ($H_2O$) from the rain to make their food, and they add oxygen ($O_2$) and water vapor to the atmosphere. **(23)**

A huge rain forest tree can live for hundreds of years, and a single leaf can remain on a tree for well over a year. Nonetheless, all living things eventually die, and the essential minerals and other chemicals that make up the bodies of trees, shrubs, vines, insects, parrots, monkeys, and all else are recycled in a process called *decomposition*. Many soils in tropical rain forests do not contain very much in the way of vital minerals, such as calcium, potassium, or magnesium. This is because recycling is so rapid and efficient in tropical forests that the minerals are reclaimed by plants before they can be "lost" into soil or washed away by heavy rainfall.

water

falling
leaves

leaf litter

shallow topsoil

water and nutrients

14

The work of decomposition is done mostly by the many kinds of **fungi** and **bacteria (24)** that inhabit rain forests. Bacteria are one-celled organisms so tiny that they can be seen only with a microscope. They live by the trillions in rain forests and are quick to feed on the bodies of all dead organisms, from leaves to birds.

Fungi (a single one is called a *fungus)* are much like plants, but they lack green chlorophyll. Fungi grow abundantly in tropical soils as dense networks of threadlike strands that grow in and around dead wood, leaves, and animals. Mushrooms, as well as bracket mushrooms, which grow on trees, are the spore-containing "fruit" of various fungi. They can be quite colorful.

Both fungi and bacteria take in energy by breaking down dead things. In this way, the minerals locked up in the dead leaves and animal bodies are released back onto the forest floor. Tree roots, usually on or near the soil surface, quickly absorb the minerals and use them in making new tissue.

Some fungi live in the soil next to tree roots, helping the roots take up minerals so that both the tree and the fungi benefit. Such fungi, which have the tongue-twisting name *mycorrhiza* (pronounced *my kuh RY zuh*), also grow within the roots of orchids and bromeliads (pages 9, 16), making it possible for these air plants to survive without soil.

The pattern of recycling in a rain forest, where nutrients move among the different plants and animals, always being reused, is quite delicate. Sometimes, when rain forests are cut down, this recycling system is so disturbed that the forest cannot grow back.

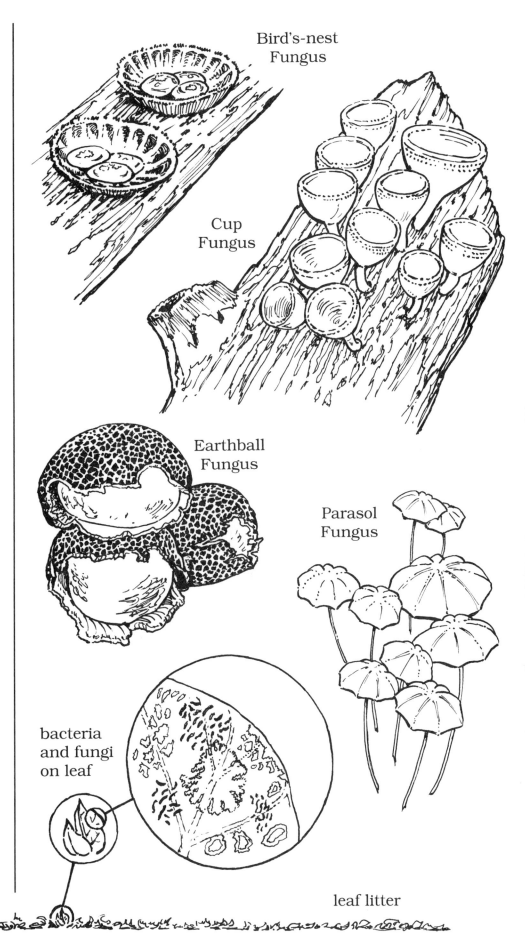

Bird's-nest
Fungus

Cup
Fungus

Earthball
Fungus

Parasol
Fungus

bacteria
and fungi
on leaf

leaf litter

15

## 25. Inside a bromeliad

slug

dart-
poison frog
and tadpoles

spider

crab

mosquito
larvae

## Inside a Bromeliad

A **bromeliad (25)** is a kind of tropical air plant, or epiphyte, that grows abundantly on rain forest trees. Not all of the nearly 2000 species of bromeliads are air plants — the familiar and delicious pineapple is a bromeliad but is firmly rooted in the ground.

Many kinds of rain forest animals live inside the cup of a bromeliad's leaves, including tree frogs and their tadpoles, spiders, slugs, mosquitos, and crabs. In this sense, bromeliads are really miniature rain forest habitats. The rain forest has such a great number of species partly because so many kinds of small animals manage to crowd into such tiny habitats as bromeliads.

Bromeliad leaves are thick and waxy, and their edges are lined with small, sharp spines. The leaves overlap so that the entire plant is somewhat like a cup that can trap rain water. Through very fine hairs on its leaves, the plant can absorb valuable minerals as well as the water itself. The thin roots of the plant grow among the mosses and lichens that normally carpet tropical tree branches.

The bromeliad flowers grow from a long stalk and are often bright red, attracting humming-birds (page 33). The brightly colored little Euphonia tanager (pages 38-39) often hides its tiny nest among bromeliad leaves.

16

## Tropical House Plants

*Some of our most prized house plants are native to the tropics, and often grow in great abundance along roadsides and in open fields.*

The **Bird-of-Paradise Flower,** which first grew in Africa but is now found widely in tropical America, is a member of the Heliconia family (page 12). It has long paddle-shaped leaves and bright orange flowers with petals shaped like spearheads. **(26)**

**Anthurium,** also called Flamingo Flower, is bright shiny red with a long pale stalk called a spadix. Many kinds of anthuriums grow in the American tropics. Some have white, pink, or yellow flowers. Anthuriums grow along forest edges and attract hummingbirds and bees as pollinators. **(27)**

**Amaryllis** is another bright red flower, and a very large one. A member of the lily family, Amaryllis originated in South American rain forests but is now widely kept as an ornamental plant grown from a bulb. **(28)**

**Hibiscus** flowers are easy to recognize because of the long central pistil that extends like a stalk from the cluster of large red petals. Hibiscus is native to the Old World, with some kinds originating in Africa, others in China. **(29)**

**Bougainvillea** is a native of Brazil that is now common on many Caribbean islands. Flowers grow in long, deep red sprays that seem to cover the thorny branches. **(30)**

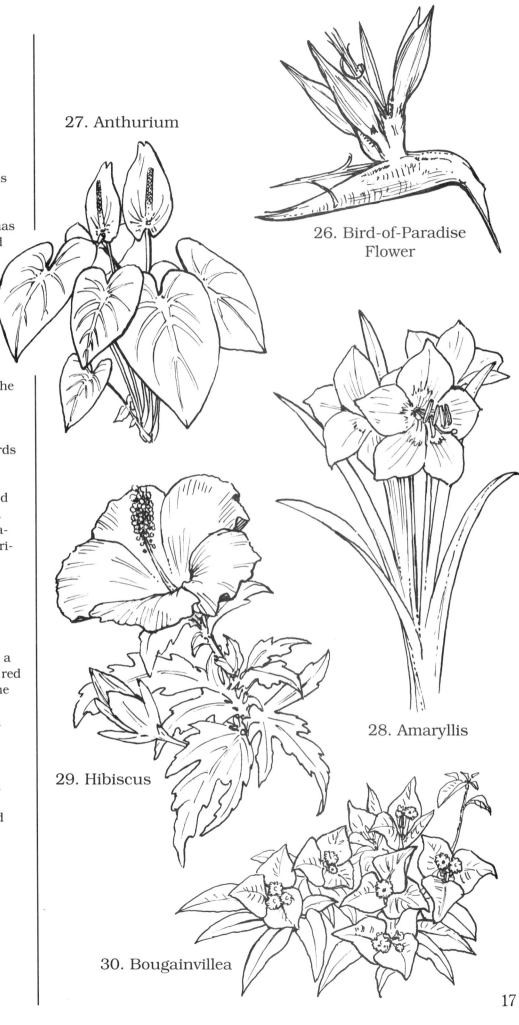

27. Anthurium

26. Bird-of-Paradise Flower

28. Amaryllis

29. Hibiscus

30. Bougainvillea

17

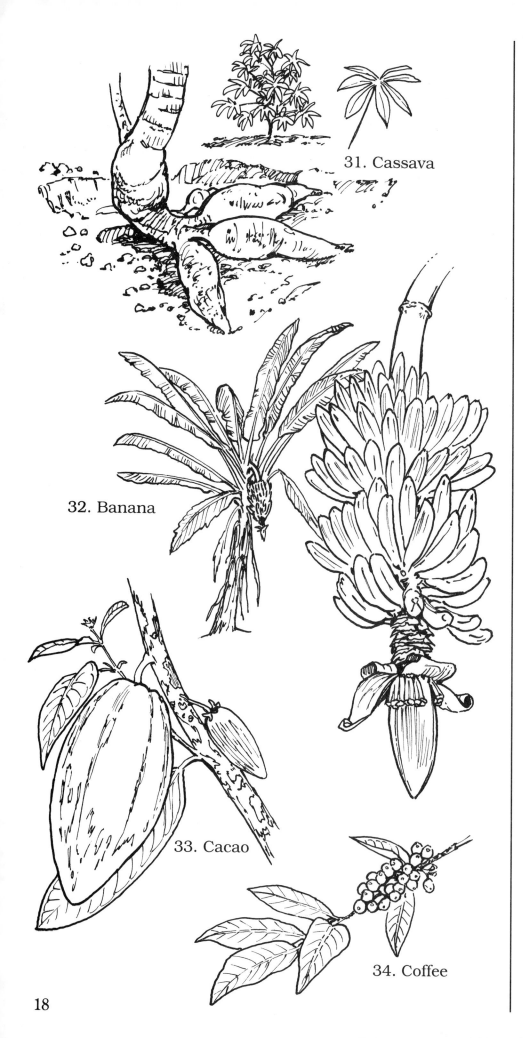

31. Cassava

32. Banana

33. Cacao

34. Coffee

## Food Plants from the Tropics

*Many kinds of useful plants are tropical in origin, including some of our favorite food plants.*

Most North Americans are not familiar with **cassava,** also called manioc, but it is perhaps the most important food plant of the rain forest peoples. Its thick root is highly nutritious. Amerindians make bread from the cassava root. It is also used to make tapioca. In some places cassava root contains cyanide, a deadly poison, and the root must be washed and squeezed to eliminate the poison. **(31)**

**Bananas** originated in the Old World tropics, in India and Myanmar, and were introduced into the New World tropics in 1516. The large, arrow-shaped flower head is very distinctive, as are the huge, long leaves. Tropical farmers usually keep banana trees near their houses to provide a tasty dessert. Plantains, a kind of banana, are sliced and fried like potato chips. **(32)**

Chocolate, perhaps the most popular candy in the world, is tropical in origin. It comes from the **Cacao** tree, a small tree of the shady rain forest understory. Chocolate is prepared from the tree's football-shaped red gourds, the seed-containing fruits that grow directly from the main trunk. **(33)**

**Coffee** is also an understory shrub, but one that prefers cool mountainsides rather than lowland rain forest. Usually, coffee is planted among taller trees because the plants require shade to grow best. Coffee flowers are white and are pollinated by the light winds that penetrate through the forest. Coffee "beans" are the seeds of the red coffee fruits, which are called cherries. The coffee we drink is made from roasted beans. **(34)**

**Breadfruit** is immediately recognized by its large, green, knobby-skinned fruits and dark green leaves with deep notches. Breadfruit trees are native to Polynesia, and were imported to the American tropics to produce food for slaves. The beautiful tree is still widely planted, and its energy-rich fruit is eaten fried, boiled, or baked. **(35)**

**Mango** is one of the most common and delicious fruits of the tropics. The plant is native to India and Myanmar but has been grown in the American tropics since it was first brought by Spanish and Portuguese colonists. Mango flowers are tiny, and many cluster on a single branch. The tasty fruit, which hangs from a long stalk, ranges in color from yellow to green to red. **(36)**

**Coconut palms** abound in the world's tropics, though no one is certain where the plant originated. The hardy nut, encased in a tough husk, can float for months on the ocean, taking root wherever it washes ashore. The white meat of the nut is eaten fresh or can be dried for cooking. Inside the hollow center is refreshing coconut "milk." **(37)**

**Sugar Cane** is one of the most economically important tropical crops. It is a tall grass that probably first grew in New Guinea. Flowers look like feathery plumes. Sugar is extracted by crushing the stems and processing the pulp. Molasses and rum are made from Sugar Cane. **(38)**

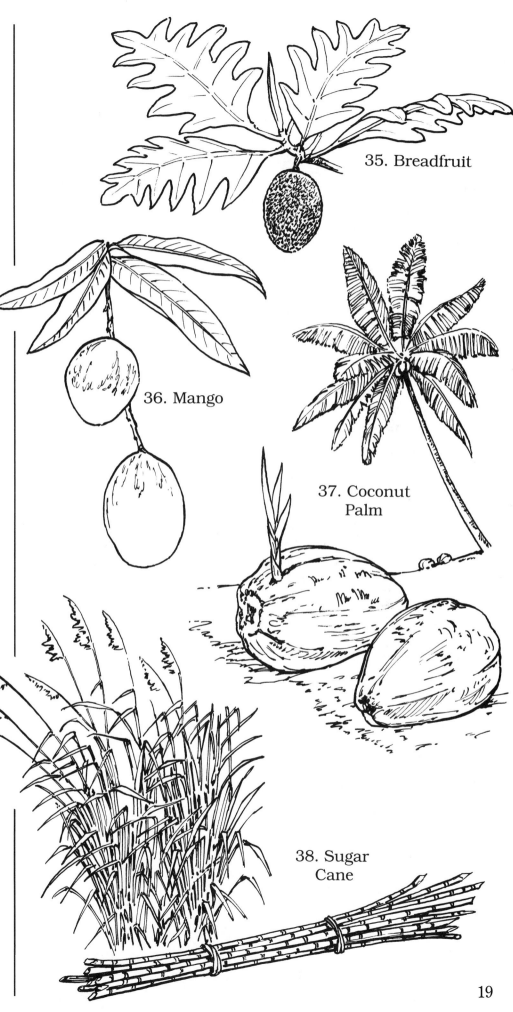

35. Breadfruit

36. Mango

37. Coconut Palm

38. Sugar Cane

39. Red Howler

40. Black-handed
Spider Monkey

41. Woolly
Monkey

42. Brown-fronted Capuchin

## Rain Forest Mammals

*There are 64 species of monkeys in the rain forests of Central and South America. They range in size from the baboon-sized howlers and woolly monkeys to the tiny Pygmy Marmoset, a creature barely larger than a mouse. Many, but not all, have prehensile tails, which means the tail can be wrapped around objects like tree branches. Most monkeys eat fruits, buds, and leaves.*

Howler monkeys are known for their jaguarlike roars, a rain forest sound that, once heard, is not soon forgotten. Male howlers have an enlarged throat sac that makes their roars much louder. Troops of howlers roar to stake out their territories, warning all other troops not to intrude. The **Red Howler,** shown here, is uniformly reddish. **(39)**

Spider monkeys look like thin versions of howlers. They have long, slender limbs and are among the most agile of all monkeys. A large one will weigh only about 14 pounds. Troops number around 30-35 animals, mostly females and young. Spider monkeys move through the rain forest canopy in search of fruits. The **Black-handed Spider Monkey,** shown here, has black arms, legs, and head and a reddish brown body. It lives in Panama. **(40)**

**Woolly monkeys** are named for their dense fur. They vary in color from black to gray-brown to reddish. Woolly monkeys live in the Amazon Basin and do not get as far north as the Central American jungles. Like spider monkeys, they feed heavily on fruits, often picking them while hanging upside down, anchored by their prehensile tails. **(41)**

Capuchin monkeys are small and cute, and are familiar performers in circuses. Several kinds of capuchins range through the Amazon Basin and Central

America, and all feed on fruits, leaves, and various insects. The **Brown-fronted Capuchin** is shown here. Capuchin troops tend to move quickly, making considerable noise as they dash through the rain forest canopy. **(42)**

The **Pygmy Marmoset,** at a mere 6 inches long, is the smallest of the monkeys. Marmosets live in troops, scurrying like squirrels among the vines and trees of the forest edge. Pygmys are rich brown, almost yellowish, and, like all marmosets, they have a long tail that is not prehensile. Marmosets eat fruits and insects but also chew into bark and eat the energy-rich gum shed from the tree. **(43)**

The **Cotton-topped Tamarin** is quite unmistakable. This white-headed gnome of northern South American rain forests is at once recognized by its black face and outrageous tufted white head. Tamarins live in troops of up to a dozen animals and feed on fruits, buds, and insects. **(44)**

The odd **Night Monkey** is well named — it is the only monkey more active at night than in daytime. Night Monkeys have large eyes outlined in white, giving them the common name of Owl Monkey. Like owls, Night Monkeys are also fond of hooting on moonlit nights. They eat fruits, flower nectar, and insects. **(45)**

Perhaps the oddest American monkey is the rare **Red Uakari** (pronounced *wah KAYR ee*). This long-haired, stubby-tailed denizen of the Amazon has a naked face of brilliant red skin! Its utterly bald head adds to its unforgettable appearance. Though normally the fur is reddish, one kind has all white fur. Uakaris feed on leaves, fruits, insects (including hairy caterpillars), and seeds. They live along rivers, in forests that flood every year. **(46)**

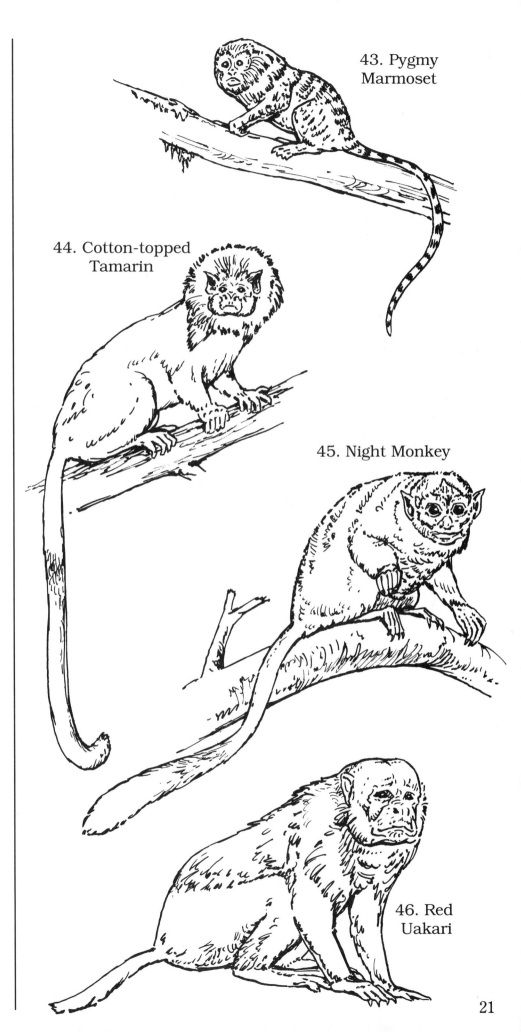

43. Pygmy Marmoset

44. Cotton-topped Tamarin

45. Night Monkey

46. Red Uakari

21

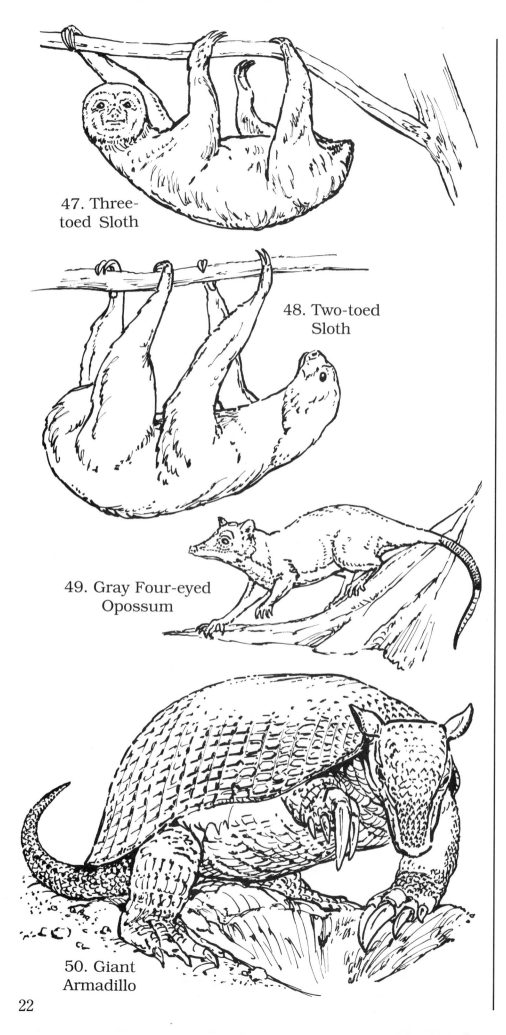

47. Three-toed Sloth

48. Two-toed Sloth

49. Gray Four-eyed Opossum

50. Giant Armadillo

Sloths somewhat resemble monkeys, and they are equally fond of trees. There are two kinds of sloths, and to tell them apart, you must count the toes on their front feet. The **Three-toed Sloth (47)** has three claws, whereas the **Two-toed Sloth (48)** has but two. They use their long claws as hooks to hang from branches. Sloths are very slow moving, not at all active like monkeys. Their bodies are made for hanging upside down, not for walking, and they have a hard time getting around on the ground. Sloths are not very tidy. Because they live in rain forests, their fur tends to be damp, and green algae grows on the fur. This gives the otherwise golden-brown sloth a distinctly green appearance — a good disguise for an animal that lives in the treetops.

*Marsupials* are mammals whose young are born tiny and develop inside a pouch on their mother. Marsupials are quite common in the American tropics. They include several dozen opossum species, such as this one, the **Gray Four-Eyed Opossum.** It is named for the prominent white spots over its eyes, which give it a "four-eyed" appearance. This 10-inch animal can be found in the rain forest canopy or scurrying along the forest floor in search of insects and fruit. It frequents the river's edge, hunting frogs. **(49)**

Several armadillo species inhabit South America. The one shown here is by far the largest, measuring 5 feet in length and weighing up to 130 pounds. It is quite worthy of its name, **Giant Armadillo.** This large slow-moving animal is found throughout the Amazon Basin but is rarely seen because it is active at night and travels alone. It uses its long front claws to dig into termite and ant nests. Its tough bony skin helps protect it from predators such as the Jaguar. **(50)**

The **Kinkajou** is a large-eyed, nocturnal member of the raccoon family. Similar in size to a monkey, it is a rich reddish color and has a long prehensile tail. Kinkajous scurry about the forest treetops at night, and several may feed together on fruits in the same tree. They have a variety of calls, including one that sounds like sneezing. **(51)**

As Kinkajous patrol the treetops, **Coatimundis** roam the rain forest floor. A Coati resembles a slender raccoon with a long, tapered snout and a longer, less bushy tail. Its body is reddish brown, and its tail has black rings. Coatis lack the raccoon's face mask. Coatis travel about in small groups (usually holding their tails straight up), eating a variety of foods. They also climb trees. **(52)**

The **Tayra** is a member of the weasel family, and is a long, slender animal. It can be all black, or it may have a tan head and chest. The Tayra's body is 2 feet long, and its tail is about 18 inches long and somewhat bushy. Tayras are active hunters by day, searching for small mammals and insects. They often are seen near human dwellings as well as in rain forests. **(53)**

The **Bush Dog** is somewhat similar to the Tayra in size and overall shape, but it has a shorter, less bushy tail. With its short snout and little ears, the Bush Dog resembles a stubby fox. Coat color is reddish on the head, with black legs and tail and black on the rump. Small groups of Bush Dogs travel by day in search of prey such as Pacas (page 26). They are rare in most places, and few travelers are lucky enough to see them. **(54)**

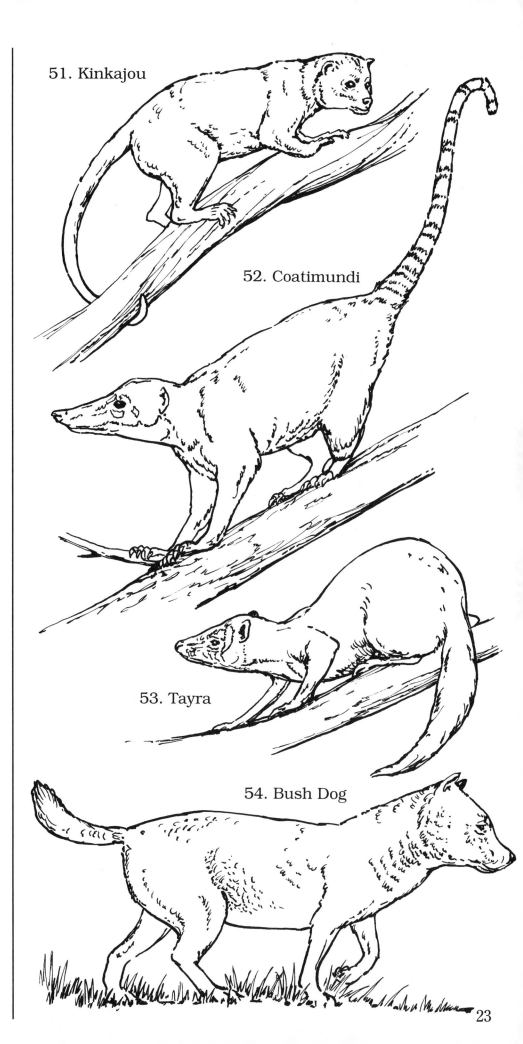

51. Kinkajou

52. Coatimundi

53. Tayra

54. Bush Dog

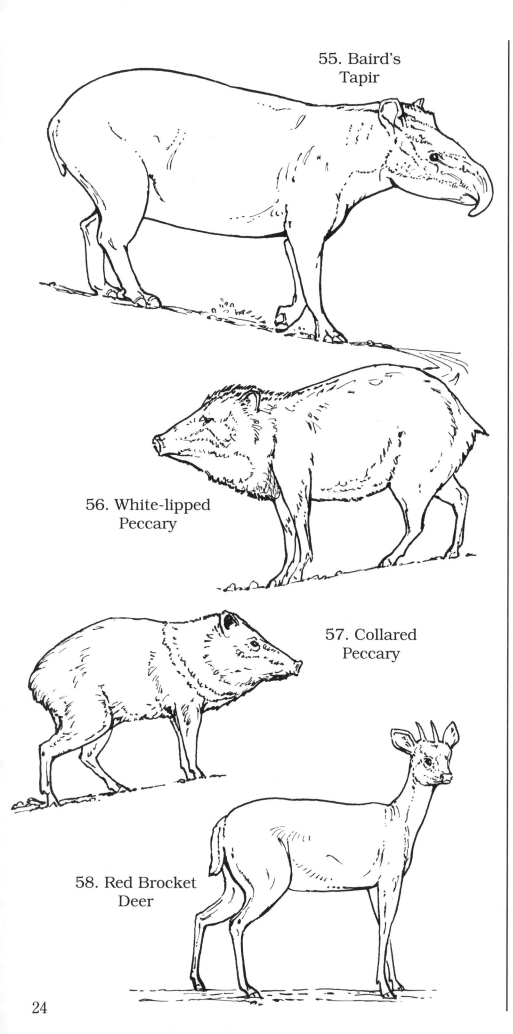

## 55. Baird's Tapir

## 56. White-lipped Peccary

## 57. Collared Peccary

## 58. Red Brocket Deer

*Unlike the vast African plains, the tropical American rain forest is home to few large hoofed animals. Those that do live there are often somewhat secretive, nocturnal, and hard to find.*

Among these hoofed animals is the **Baird's Tapir,** one of only four tapir species in the world. Tapirs are related to horses and rhinoceroses. They are large, stocky, and almost hairless, colored grayish black with pale undersides. Juveniles have white stripes along their sides. Tapirs have a short, flexible snout that they use to grab plants, much the same way an elephant uses its trunk. They often feed along rivers and marshy areas. The thick neck and short mane helps them move through dense brush. **(55)**

There are two species of peccaries, the **White-lipped Peccary (56)** and the **Collared Peccary (57),** both resembling pigs. Unlike true pigs, however, peccaries do not have tusks — they have straight, sharp teeth that they use for defense and in rooting up food. Peccaries are covered by dense bristly hairs. They travel in herds of anywhere from 6 to over 100 animals. Collared Peccaries, which also occur in Texas, Arizona, and New Mexico, weigh about 65 pounds and are grayish black with a white shoulder stripe. White-lipped Peccaries are larger, more black, with a white throat. Peccaries feed much like pigs and eat a wide variety of foods.

Several deer species occur in the American tropics, among them the **Red Brocket Deer.** Smaller than the familiar White-tailed Deer (which also occurs in the tropics), brocket deer have small antlers, and their rump is higher than their shoulders. This species is rich chestnut red, with a grayish neck. Brocket deer feed heavily on fruits and are mostly solitary. They can be found throughout the forest. **(58)**

The **Giant Anteater** is an unmistakable resident of rain forest and open grassland. Including its long, shaggy tail, this animal reaches a length of 5 feet, making it easily the largest anteater. It uses its long, curved front claws to dig into ant and termite nests. From its narrow, funnel-shaped head, it can extend its sticky tongue 20 inches into the mounds to reach the nutritious insects. The coat color is gray-brown, with a black throat and black stripe on the shoulder. When threatened, the animal rears up and uses its front claws to defend itself. **(59)**

The **Tamandua** or Lesser Anteater is only about one-third the size of its giant cousin. It dwells in trees, using its prehensile tail to help it move among the branches. Its fur is yellowish tan with blackish sides. Tamanduas feed on ants and termites, digging into the nests with their sharp front claws. During the dry season they tend to eat many termites, which have more water in them than ants. **(60)**

The little **Silky Anteater** is also called the Pygmy Anteater because of its small size, just 1.5 feet. This secretive animal lives among the vines and branches of tall trees and is active mostly at night. During the daytime it sleeps, curled into a tight ball tucked among the vines. Its dense woolly fur, which feels quite silky, is gold-yellow with a bright sheen. **(61)**

The **Prehensile-tailed Porcupine,** as its name implies, uses its long tail as a fifth limb for getting around the rain forest canopy. Like its North American cousin, it is well supplied with sharp spines that easily detach if the animal is molested. The overall coat color is black, sometimes brown, with gray spines. **(62)**

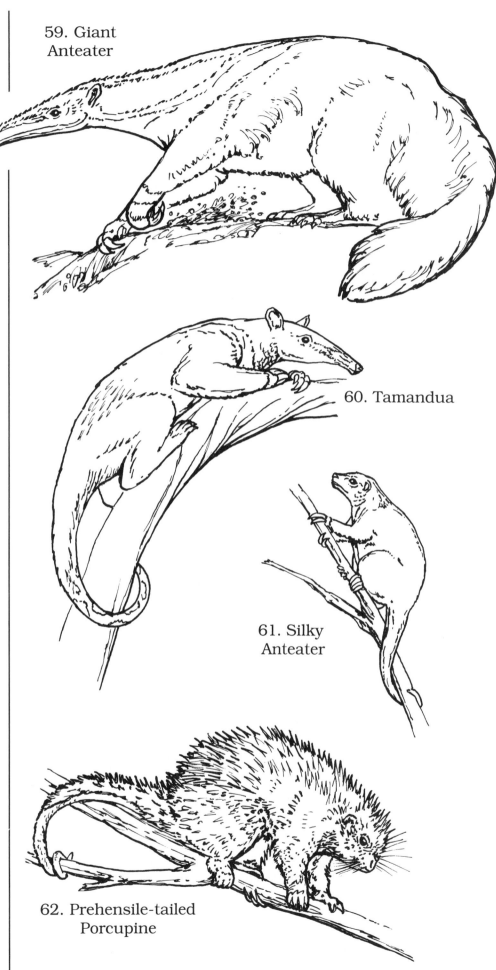

59. Giant Anteater

60. Tamandua

61. Silky Anteater

62. Prehensile-tailed Porcupine

64. Paca

63. Agouti

65. Red
squirrel

66. Variegated
Squirrel

In tropical rain forests throughout Central and South America there are two close relations of the familiar Guinea Pig. **Agoutis (63)** and **Pacas (64)** are about the size of a house cat. Both are chunky animals with long, squirrellike faces. They somewhat resemble tiny deer as they prance delicately across the forest floor. Agoutis stamp their small feet and bark loudly when startled.

Agoutis range in color from rich reddish to gray-brown. Pacas are reddish with rows of white stripes along their sides and a white belly. Agoutis and Pacas usually travel alone, though occasionally a mated pair will search for food together. Agoutis and Pacas dine on seeds, fruits, flowers, and various leaves. Both animals make burrows in which they spend most of the day. Both are hunted for food by local peoples.

It is not surprising that in a land of so many trees, there are many kinds of tree squirrels. Three species of **red squirrels** range throughout the vast Amazon Basin, and all three look very much alike. As the name implies, they are rich red, especially on the bushy tail. Red squirrels look almost identical to the familiar Gray and Fox squirrels of North America. They feed on many kinds of nuts and fruits and are particularly attracted to palm nuts. Unlike their northern cousins, tropical squirrels are wary of humans and flee if people get too close. **(65)**

The **Variegated Squirrel** is named for the fact that it comes in three color forms: gray-black, black and white, and red-black. Variegated Squirrels live high in the treetops of Central America, feeding mostly on fruits. **(66)**

*The sudden sight of an Ocelot or its larger relative, the Jaguar, is one of the most thrilling of all experiences for the tropical explorer. Cats tend to hunt for prey at night, so seeing one in daytime requires good luck. Wild cats of the tropics are often killed for their beautifully patterned fur. In many places these cats are endangered species. Wearing coats of wild cat fur should be discouraged — human vanity should not come before the life of a magnificent creature.*

The **Jaguar** is the largest tropical American cat, called El Tigre (tiger) by people of the rain forests. It is 6 feet long, weighs 300 pounds, and is patterned like the Ocelot and Margay. Jaguars prowl the rain forest, hunting prey that ranges from agoutis and peccaries to tortoises, birds, and fish. Jaguars hunt both day and night, often patrolling along rivers and beaches, sometimes using trails made by humans. Like other big cats, Jaguars are known for their loud roars. **(67)**

The **Ocelot (68)** and the **Margay (69)** look similar, a rich tan color with chestnut spots bordered by black. The Margay's markings look like spots, however, and the Ocelot's look more like stripes. At 3.5 feet long (with a 16-inch tail) and weighing 25 pounds, the Ocelot is a bit larger than the Margay. Both cats prowl the forest floor, and both can climb trees. Their diet ranges from insects to small monkeys.

The **Jaguarundi** is recognized by its slender shape and long tail. Most individuals are dark gray-brown, but some are reddish, tawny, or almost black. Jaguarundis range thoughout Central and South America and are found in grasslands and near villages, as well as within rain forests. They are more active in the daytime than other cat species. **(70)**

67. Jaguar

68. Ocelot

69. Margay

70. Jaguarundi

27

71. Scarlet Macaw

73. Hyacinth Macaw

72. Blue and Yellow Macaw

74. Military Macaw

28

## Birds of the Tropics

*There are 340 species of parrots in the world. Most are strikingly colorful, and most live in the tropics. Parrots are raucous and highly social as they go about the business of searching out and consuming fruits. They are especially fond of the seeds inside, which they crack with their unique bills. The upper part of the bill is sharply hooked, ideal for digging into fruits, and the lower part is flat and has strong muscles. The two parts work like a nutcracker to open seeds. Parrots have fleshy tongues that skillfully probe into fruits to obtain seeds. Known for their unique personalities, intelligence, and amazing abilities to mimic sounds, including human speech, parrots are much in demand for pets. As a result, the numbers of many wild parrots have been reduced.*

Among the most spectacular of the world's parrots are the big macaws, all of which are native to Central and South America. Macaws have long tails and bare skin on their faces. They fly with slow steady wingbeats. They have a loud harsh call, and flocks of macaws are often heard before they are seen.

The 35-inch-long **Scarlet Macaw** is vivid red with blue wings and a yellow wing patch. Flocks of Scarlet Macaws often can be seen flying over rivers. **(71)**

Similar in size is the **Blue and Yellow Macaw.** It has blue upper wings, back, and tail, and is brilliant yellow, almost gold, below. Like most macaws, Blue and Yellows feed heavily on palm nuts. Both the Scarlet and Blue and Yellow Macaws inhabit the Amazon Basin. **(72)**

The deep purple **Hyacinth Macaw (73)** lives south of the Amazon Basin, and the bright green **Military Macaw (74)** is found in a variety of tropical and subtropical forests from Mexico to Argentina.

The 14-inch **Red Fan Parrot** can often be seen perched atop a snag of a dead tree along the Amazon River. It is named for its bright red neck feathers, which can be ruffed out, suggesting a fan. Like most South American parrots, the Red Fan is mostly green, but with a brownish head and red bars on the breast. **(75)**

The 10-inch **Blue-headed Parrot** is well named, though its deep blue head color is often hard to see when the birds are perched high in the treetops. Blue-heads are otherwise green with red below the tail. They often are seen in flocks of 100 or more as they travel to and from their roost. Like most parrots, they nest in hollow trees. **(76)**

The 14-inch **Scarlet-fronted Parakeet** is uniformly bright green, with a deep scarlet fore-head and crown. Parakeets have long tails and a more streamlined shape than the parrots described above. Flocks of up to several hundred birds can be found throughout the Andes Mountains from Venezuela to Peru. **(77)**

Along much of the Amazon River, screeching flocks of 9-inch **Canary-winged Parakeets** are common. They are named for their bright yellow wing patches, which flash brightly when the birds fly. Canary-wings have become established in Miami, Florida, and can often be seen in parks around the city. **(78)**

The chunky 9-inch **Black-headed Parrot** is at once recog-nized by its black cap and colorful golden-yellow face. It has a pale breast and is bright yellow below the tail. Black-heads often perch atop a palm or other tree and slowly spread their wings while calling a loud "KLEEK!" **(79)**

75. Red Fan Parrot

76. Blue-headed Parrot

77. Scarlet-fronted Parakeet

78. Canary-winged Parakeet

79. Black-headed Parrot

80. Resplendent Quetzal

81. Slaty-tailed Trogon

82. Violaceous Trogon

83. Green Jay

Somewhat parrotlike in appearance are the 40 species of trogons and quetzals. A trogon often sits upright, quite still, with its tail pointed down, then suddenly the bird darts out and snatches an insect or a fruit. Males are more colorful than females, but both sexes are clothed in soft metallic colors. Trogons nest in tree holes, and some species dig into termite mounds or wasp nests, which they use as nesting sites.

Perhaps the most magnificently plumaged bird of the American tropics is the **Resplendent Quetzal,** which lives in high mountain forests often densely covered by clouds. This species is found from southern Mexico to Panama. The Resplendent Quetzal is bright green with a deep red belly and white below the tail. The bird itself is 14 inches long, and the male has 25-inch-long green tail plumes that stream out behind as the bird flies. **(80)**

The **Slaty-tailed Trogon** is colored in muted red and green, with black below the tail. This species has a bright orange bill and a red ring around its eye. Although large (12 inches), the Slaty-tail is hard to see, as it perches quite still in the deep shade of the rain forest. **(81)**

Many trogon species have bright yellow bellies, and the 9-inch **Violaceous Trogon** is one of the most widespread from this group, ranging from Mexico through the Amazon Basin. Males have a shimmering violet head accented by a yellow eye ring. The tail is mostly white, with black bars. **(82)**

Unrelated to the trogons but just as colorful is the 12-inch **Green Jay.** This gaudy bird is bright green above, yellow below, with a blue head and black cheeks and throat. You can find families of Green Jays in forests from southern Texas all the way to the Bolivian Andes. **(83)**

Motmots are jay-sized birds that are colored subtle shades of green and reddish brown. Most kinds of motmots, including the two shown here, have raquet-like tails that they swing slowly from side to side as they perch in the rain forest understory. The largest motmot is the 18-inch **Rufous Motmot (84),** named for its reddish head and breast. It has a black mask. The **Blue-crowned Motmot (85),** 15 inches, is found along forest edges, gardens, and plantations, as well as in rain forests. Motmots eat large insects and fruits.

Jacamars are often found along streams or forest edges, where they sit quietly, then dart out and snap up insects. The **Great Jacamar** (12 inches) has a metallic green head, wings, and tail, and a reddish breast. Its long bill is black. Jacamars and motmots nest in tunnels that they dig in embankments. **(86)**

The **Black-fronted Nunbird** (11 inches) is uniformly charcoal black with a bright red bill. It sits upright in the forest understory and captures insects with a snap of its bill. Nunbirds sometimes follow troops of monkeys, preying on insects they stir up. Nunbirds also build tunnel nests in earth banks. **(87)**

The husky 9-inch **White-necked Puffbird** is one of 30 puffbird species, all of which occur in the American tropics. This boldly patterned black and white bird is often overlooked by bird watchers as it sits utterly motionless atop a tall tree. A puffbird will fly out and capture an insect in mid-air, then return to its perch, often beating the insect with its bill before eating it. **(88)**

84. Rufous Motmot

85. Blue-crowned Motmot

86. Great Jacamar

87. Black-fronted Nunbird

88. White-necked Puffbird

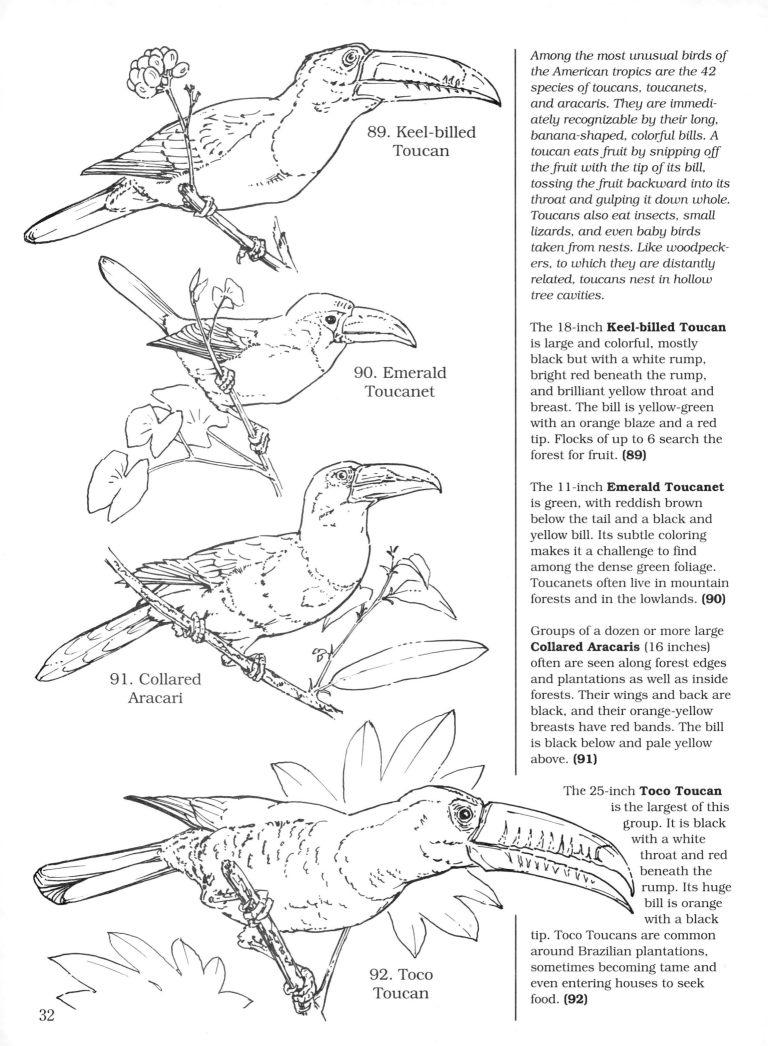

89. Keel-billed Toucan

90. Emerald Toucanet

91. Collared Aracari

92. Toco Toucan

Among the most unusual birds of the American tropics are the 42 species of toucans, toucanets, and aracaris. They are immediately recognizable by their long, banana-shaped, colorful bills. A toucan eats fruit by snipping off the fruit with the tip of its bill, tossing the fruit backward into its throat and gulping it down whole. Toucans also eat insects, small lizards, and even baby birds taken from nests. Like woodpeckers, to which they are distantly related, toucans nest in hollow tree cavities.

The 18-inch **Keel-billed Toucan** is large and colorful, mostly black but with a white rump, bright red beneath the rump, and brilliant yellow throat and breast. The bill is yellow-green with an orange blaze and a red tip. Flocks of up to 6 search the forest for fruit. **(89)**

The 11-inch **Emerald Toucanet** is green, with reddish brown below the tail and a black and yellow bill. Its subtle coloring makes it a challenge to find among the dense green foliage. Toucanets often live in mountain forests and in the lowlands. **(90)**

Groups of a dozen or more large **Collared Aracaris** (16 inches) often are seen along forest edges and plantations as well as inside forests. Their wings and back are black, and their orange-yellow breasts have red bands. The bill is black below and pale yellow above. **(91)**

The 25-inch **Toco Toucan** is the largest of this group. It is black with a white throat and red beneath the rump. Its huge bill is orange with a black tip. Toco Toucans are common around Brazilian plantations, sometimes becoming tame and even entering houses to seek food. **(92)**

All of the world's 330 species of hummingbirds are found in the Americas. Using their long slender bills, hummingbirds probe flowers for nectar. They can hover in mid-air, beating their wings up to 80 times per second! Many of the hummingbirds' colors are iridescent, shining brilliantly in the sun. The beauty of hummingbirds is revealed in their names: woodstars, emeralds, and goldenthroats, to name a few.

The brownish, 6-inch **Long-tailed Hermit** flies swiftly through the understory and around the forest edges, probing flowers such as Heliconias (page 12). Hermits are "trapliners," meaning they visit flowers along an established route. **(93)**

Another long-tailed hummingbird is the 7-inch **Long-tailed Sylph,** which lives along rain forest borders. Like many hummers, males are more colorful than females, and only males have long tails. Males are bright green with turquoise streamerlike tails. **(94)**

At only 2.7 inches, the **Spangled Coquette** is one of the smallest hummingbirds. It is instantly recognizable by its orange-red crest, bright green throat, and short, bright orange bill. This tiny hummer often feeds on flowering trees high in the rain forest canopy. **(95)**

Many people believe the 3-inch **Ruby-topaz Hummingbird** to be the most beautiful of all the hummingbirds. Males are rich chestnut with a glittering orange throat and bright red head. This hummer lives in dry forests and forest edges. **(96)**

The 4-inch **Fork-tailed Wood-nymph** has a bright green throat and deep violet breast and belly. Its forked tail is deep blue. Like many hummers, it is often territorial and will drive away other birds. **(97)**

93. Long-tailed Hermit

94. Long-tailed Sylph

95. Spangled Coquette

96. Ruby-topaz Hummingbird

97. Fork-tailed Woodnymph

33

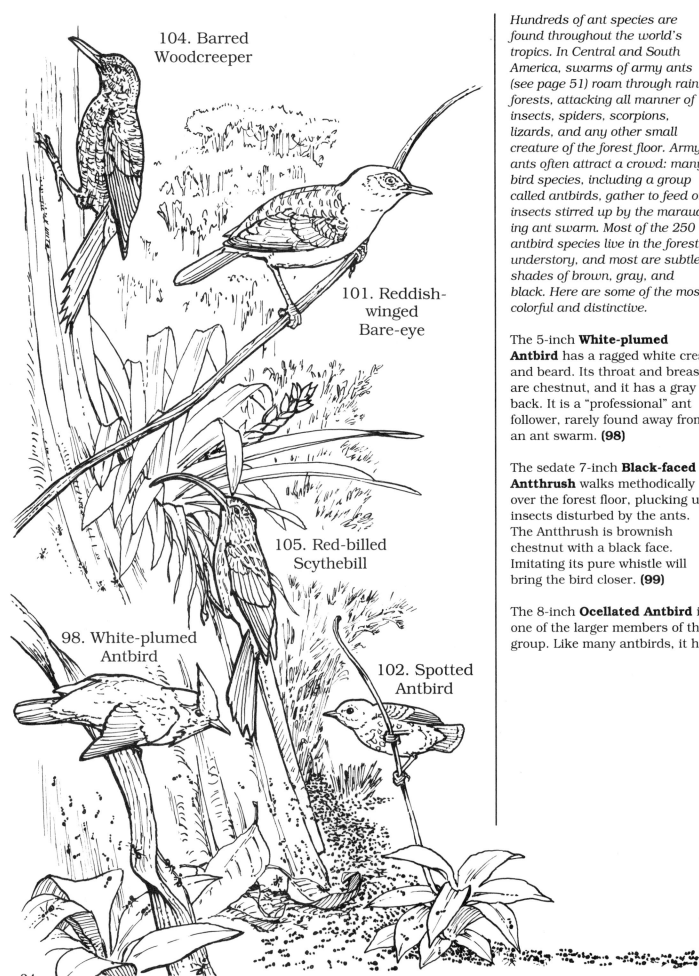

104. Barred
Woodcreeper

101. Reddish-
winged
Bare-eye

105. Red-billed
Scythebill

98. White-plumed
Antbird

102. Spotted
Antbird

Hundreds of ant species are found throughout the world's tropics. In Central and South America, swarms of army ants (see page 51) roam through rain forests, attacking all manner of insects, spiders, scorpions, lizards, and any other small creature of the forest floor. Army ants often attract a crowd: many bird species, including a group called antbirds, gather to feed on insects stirred up by the marauding ant swarm. Most of the 250 antbird species live in the forest understory, and most are subtle shades of brown, gray, and black. Here are some of the most colorful and distinctive.

The 5-inch **White-plumed Antbird** has a ragged white crest and beard. Its throat and breast are chestnut, and it has a gray back. It is a "professional" ant follower, rarely found away from an ant swarm. **(98)**

The sedate 7-inch **Black-faced Antthrush** walks methodically over the forest floor, plucking up insects disturbed by the ants. The Antthrush is brownish chestnut with a black face. Imitating its pure whistle will bring the bird closer. **(99)**

The 8-inch **Ocellated Antbird** is one of the larger members of the group. Like many antbirds, it has bare skin around its eyes, in this case colored blue. The throat is black, the neck and breast chestnut, and the wings and back brown with black spots. **(100)**

The **Reddish-winged Bare-Eye** is similar, a black antbird with reddish brown on its wings and a bright red patch of bare skin around the eyes. **(101)**

The 4-inch **Spotted Antbird** is one of the smaller members of the group. Males have a white breast with black spots. **(102)**

The 7-inch **Rufous-crowned Antpitta** is oddly shaped. It stands upright on long legs and has an extremely short tail. It is secretive, and is more often heard than seen. **(103)**

Other birds besides antbirds often follow army ant swarms. Woodcreepers, such as the 11-inch **Barred Woodcreeper (104)** and the 9-inch **Red-billed Scythebill (105),** use their long bills to probe tree bark and bromeliads for hidden insects and spiders. The tiny 5-inch **Plain Xenops (106)** often hangs upside down like a chickadee while searching leaves for insects. The big 14-inch, black and red **Lineated Woodpecker (107)** drills bark in search of grubs.

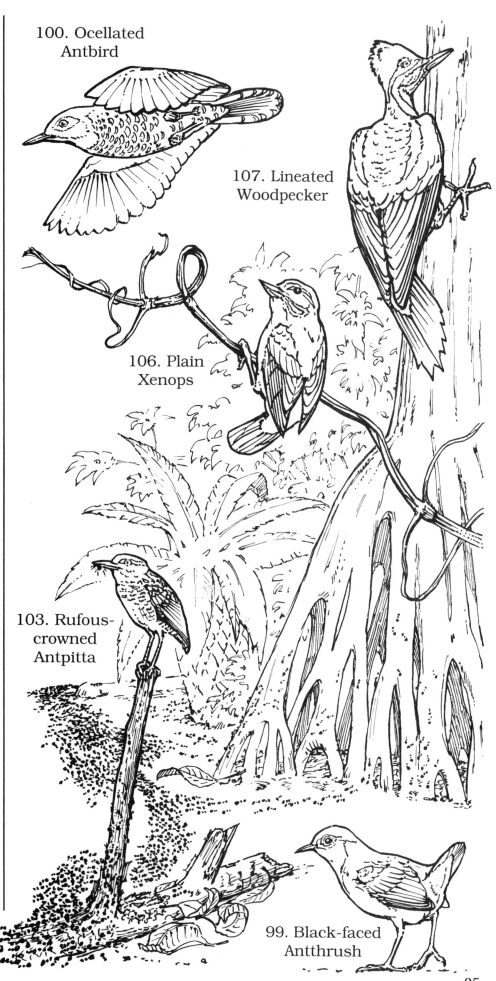

100. Ocellated Antbird

107. Lineated Woodpecker

106. Plain Xenops

103. Rufous-crowned Antpitta

99. Black-faced Antthrush

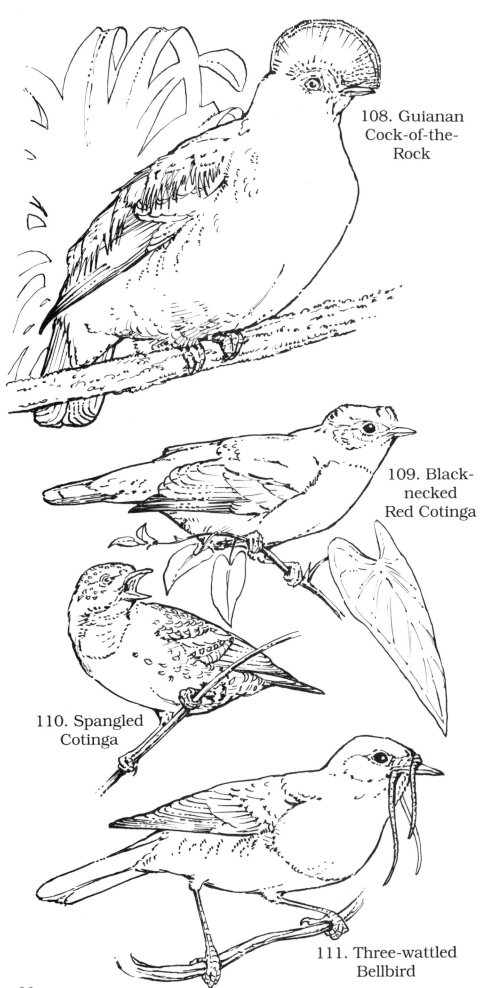

108. Guianan Cock-of-the-Rock

109. Black-necked Red Cotinga

110. Spangled Cotinga

111. Three-wattled Bellbird

*Many rain forest birds feed almost entirely on fruit. Among this group are some of the rain forest's most splendidly colored species.*

The husky 13-inch male **Guianan Cock-of-the-Rock** is brilliant orange with black wings and tail. Groups of up to 40 males gather in chosen areas in the shady rain forest interior to court females, which are much duller in color. **(108)**

Boldly patterned in scarlet and black is the 9-inch **Black-necked Red Cotinga,** a resident of the deep rain forest understory. Though quite colorful, this species is rarely seen and not well studied. **(109)**

The 8-inch **Spangled Cotinga** is glittering turquoise with a bright purple throat. This bird of the Amazonian rain forest often perches high atop the trees. Females are speckled brown, far less colorful than the gaudy males. **(110)**

Among the more odd-looking tropical birds is the 12-inch **Three-wattled Bellbird.** Bellbirds are named for their pealing calls that ring through the forest. Males are chestnut with a white head and have three black wattles hanging from the base of the bill. Females are yellowish green. **(111)**

Looking somewhat like a crow with a crested head, the 20-inch, all-black **Amazonian Umbrella-bird** sits high atop trees along the Amazon River. This bird is named for its odd, umbrellalike crest. It has a long "beard" of black feathers hanging from its throat. **(112)**

The 7-inch **Orange-breasted Fruiteater** is named for its habit of feeding heavily on berries as it roams through Andean cloud forests. Males are green with a black head, red bill, and bright orange throat. Females are green with some yellow on the breast. **(113)**

*Among the smallest and most colorful tropical birds are the 60 species of manakins. Males are usually far more brightly colored than females, and males often gather together to court females, somewhat like the Cock-of-the-Rock. The males of some kinds perform elaborate dances to attract females. The three male manakins shown here are all about 4 inches long.*

The **Wire-tailed Manakin** has wiry tail plumes. The male is yellow on the throat and breast, with black wings and tail and a bright red cap. **(114)**

The **Red-capped Manakin** is glossy black with a shining scarlet head and bright white eye ring. It also has yellow "pants." **(115)**

The **White-bearded Manakin** is entirely black and white. It is named for its throat feathers, which it projects, beardlike, when performing its courtship dance. **(116)**

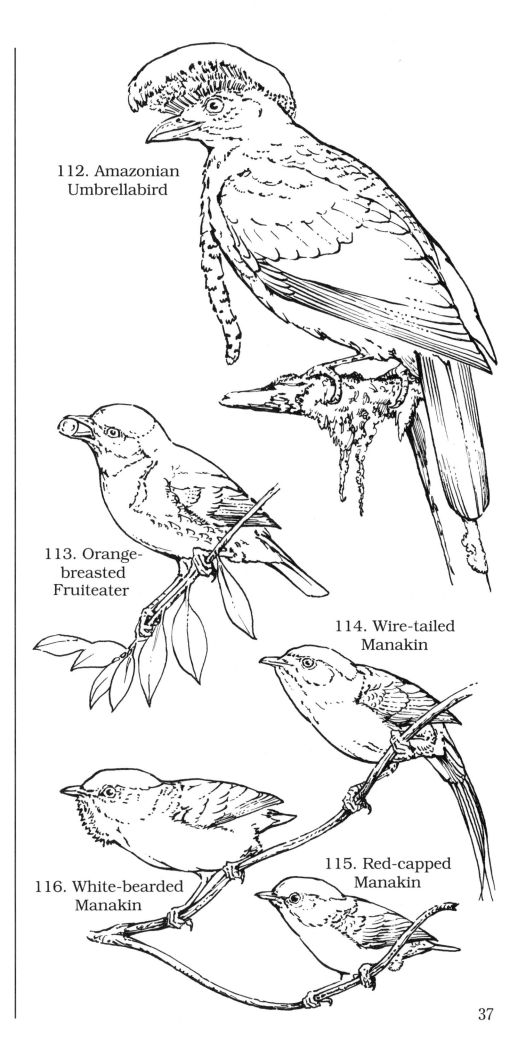

112. Amazonian Umbrellabird

113. Orange-breasted Fruiteater

114. Wire-tailed Manakin

115. Red-capped Manakin

116. White-bearded Manakin

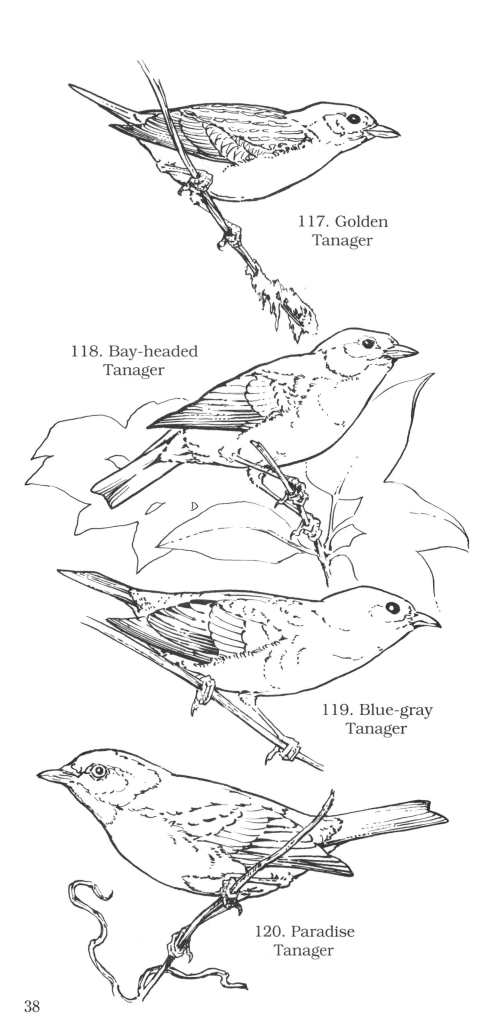

117. Golden
Tanager

118. Bay-headed
Tanager

119. Blue-gray
Tanager

120. Paradise
Tanager

Some of the 230 species of tanagers are among the brightest gems of the tropical bird world. Flocks of tanagers often roam the treetops from high Andean cloud forest to lowland tropical rain forest. They feed on both fruits and insects. The ones shown here are all about 5-6 inches long and are among the most colorful tanagers.

The **Golden Tanager** is, indeed, bright golden yellow, with a black cheek patch. It favors cloud forests and forest edges from Venezuela to Bolivia. **(117)**

The **Bay-headed Tanager** is named for its deep reddish brown head. Its back and wings are vivid green, its breast turquoise. It is found in rain forests and cloud forests from Costa Rica to the Brazilian Amazon. **(118)**

Perhaps the most widely distributed and common of the tropical tanagers is the **Blue-gray Tanager,** whose name describes its overall color. This bird is a common resident of tropical gardens, plantations, and forest edges from Mexico through Brazil. It has even been introduced into the area around Miami, Florida. **(119)**

Many people consider the **Paradise Tanager** to be the most brilliantly colored of the tanagers. Its face is shimmering green, its rump vivid red and yellow, its breast gleaming blue. It seems electric with color. Flocks search for food along the Amazon River and inside rain forests. **(120)**

High in the picturesque Andean cloud forests, flocks of **Scarlet-bellied Mountain-Tanagers** can be found. This striking red and black tanager has a blue shoulder patch, a blue rump, and a small triangle of red on its cheek. **(121)**

The unmistakable **Masked Crimson Tanager** is found in forests bordering rivers throughout the Amazon Basin. It has a crimson head and breast but is otherwise black, with the black face that gives it its name. **(122)**

Chlorophonias are chunky green tanagers of mountain forests. The **Golden-browed Chlorophonia** is named for its yellow "eyebrow." It is otherwise emerald green with a bright yellow breast and turquoise atop its head. This species is found in Costa Rica and Panama. **(123)**

Euphonias are small tanagers (4-5 inches) that sometimes nest in bromeliads (page 16). They feed on small berries, often including mistletoe. The male **Blue-hooded Euphonia** has a light blue head, black face and throat, chestnut belly and deep blue back and tail. Females are greenish yellow, with a blue head. **(124)**

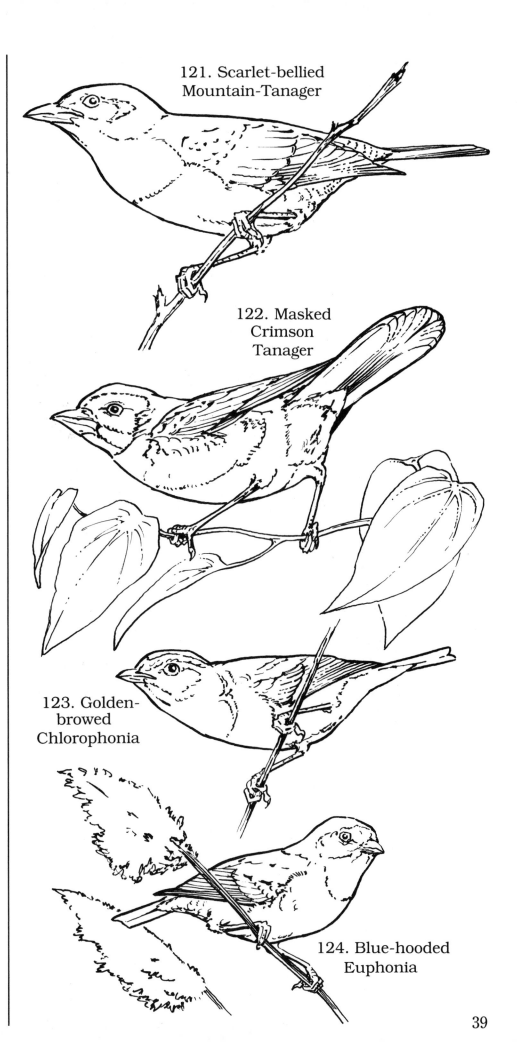

121. Scarlet-bellied Mountain-Tanager

122. Masked Crimson Tanager

123. Golden-browed Chlorophonia

124. Blue-hooded Euphonia

## 125. Dart-poison frogs

## 126. Coral snake

## 127. Heliconius butterflies

### Protective Colors

*Some rain forest animals are poisonous to predators. Many of these, like the ones on this page, are brilliantly colored. The bright patterns are an unmistakable danger signal warning predators to stay away. The warning colors are such good protection that they are mimicked by many harmless animals.*

Indians from Central America through northern South America capture **dart-poison frogs** for their poison. These small, brightly colored tree frogs have skin mucus that contains a powerful poison. This poison is used to coat darts shot from blowguns, with which the Indians hunt monkeys, birds, and other animals for food. **(125)**

There are several dozen species of **coral snakes** in the American tropics, only one of which reaches North America. All are distinctively marked with various bold bands of black, red, and yellow. (Red and yellow are the warning colors in snakes as well as traffic lights.) Related to cobras, coral snakes are extremely poisonous. Some species of nonpoisonous king snakes look very much like coral snakes. **(126)**

**Heliconius** butterflies, also called Long-winged Butterflies, usually fly slowly. Their bright colors signal the fact that most contain poisonous cyanide, making them inedible. Many other butterfly species look like Long-winged Butterflies, another case of mimicry. **(127)**

Some animals are protected by colors that make them hard to see. This is called camouflage. The species shown here are just a few of many hundreds that lurk in hiding in rain forests.

The 15-inch **Common Potoo** is patterned in various shades of brown, much like the color of bark. In daytime, this odd bird of the night perches motionless at the tip of a tree snag, looking like part of a branch. The Common Potoo has a haunting melodious whistle, given on moonlit nights. **(128)**

The **Green Vine Snake** is colored and shaped much like the tangled vines that it inhabits. This 15-inch nonpoisonous snake has a somewhat arrow-shaped head and a very slender body. If discovered, it hastily retreats. **(129)**

The **Cocoa Mort Bleu Butterfly,** also called the Owl Butterfly, has several kinds of protective coloring. At rest on a tree, the color of its wings makes it look like part of the bark. The large, owllike eyespots may distract predators from the butterfly's soft body. When taking flight the butterfly also reveals bright blue inner wings, perhaps momentarily shocking would-be predators. **(130)**

Many species of **Leaf Butterflies** can be found throughout the rain forests. These remarkable insects have wings that look exactly like dried leaves of the forest floor, even including false "holes" in the "leaves." **(131)**

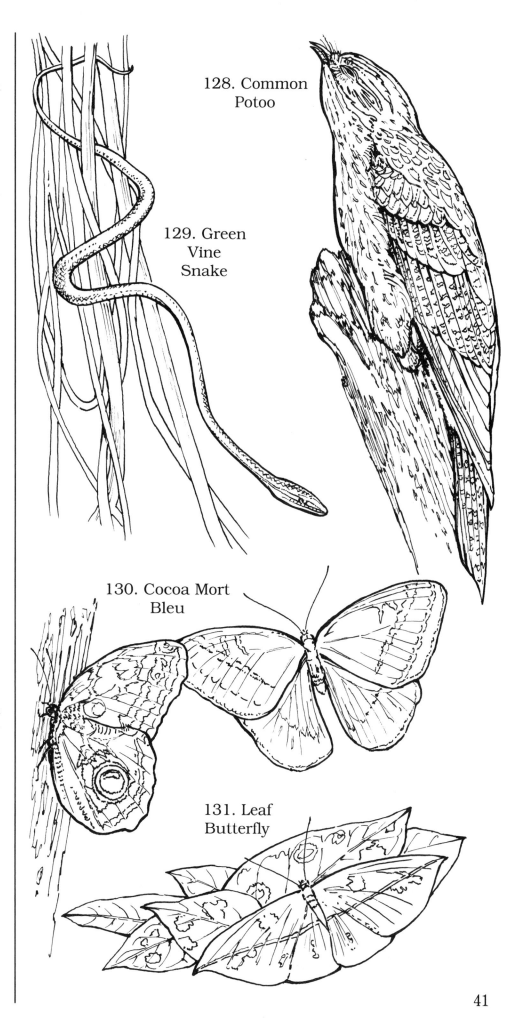

128. Common Potoo

129. Green Vine Snake

130. Cocoa Mort Bleu

131. Leaf Butterfly

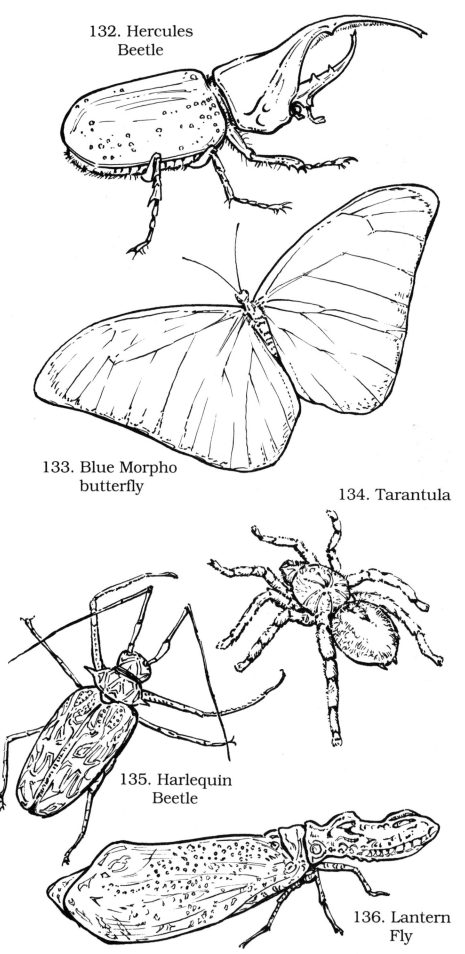

132. Hercules Beetle

133. Blue Morpho butterfly

134. Tarantula

135. Harlequin Beetle

136. Lantern Fly

## Insects and Spiders

*The tropics have no shortage of insects, spiders, and other invertebrates (animals without backbones). Some, such as those illustrated here, are impressively large and fascinating to see.*

The **Hercules Beetle** is a shiny, brownish black beetle nearly the size of a mouse. Males have large "horns" that they use as weapons to drive away other males from favored feeding sites. They can fly, and often travel at night. **(132)**

Among the most memorable sights of the tropical rain forest is one's first view of a **Blue Morpho Butterfly** as it flies through the sun-flecked understory, often near a stream or waterfall. Morphos are large, with deep blue upper wings that seem to actually glow like neon as the insect flies. When at rest, Blue Morphos fold their wings together, concealing the brilliant blue color. **(133)**

Many species of spiders crawl among fallen leaves or spin webs in the rain forest. **Tarantulas** are certainly the most imposing of this diverse group. One Amazon tarantula has a 7-inch-wide body. It is called the Bird-Eating Spider because it can actually subdue and eat small birds. Though poisonous, tarantulas are rarely dangerous to humans. **(134)**

The 3-inch **Harlequin Beetle** is recognized by its large size, long antennae, and complex pattern of red, black, and yellow. It lives in rain forest trees and feeds on sap and figs. **(135)**

The **Lantern Fly** is utterly unforgettable. Its head resembles that of an alligator, giving it the Spanish name of Mariposa Caiman, or alligator-butterfly. Though hard to spot when at rest on a tree trunk, this large insect displays bright yellow wing spots when it takes flight. **(136)**

## Rain Forest Reptiles

*Most people worry about coming upon a poisonous snake in the tropics. Indeed, dangerous snakes are present, but they are normally reclusive and very hard to find. Most snakes, including the largest, are not poisonous.*

Constrictors are a kind of nonpoisonous snake that wraps itself around its prey and squeezes, killing it by preventing it from breathing. The **Boa Constrictor,** which can reach lengths of over 10 feet, is common throughout Central and South America. It is tan with brown diamonds, remarkably good camouflage for the forest floor. **(137)**

The 6-foot-long **Emerald Tree Boa** is another snake that crushes its prey. It is bright green, with a yellow-green belly and brilliant yellow eyes. This tree-dwelling snake is as well camouflaged by its color as the brown, ground-dwelling Boa Constrictor. Boas eat birds and rodents, including Pacas and agoutis. **(138)**

Two of the most poisonous snakes found in the American tropics are the **Fer-de-Lance (139)** and the **Bushmaster (140).** Both are pit vipers, named for the pits in front of their eyes with which they detect the body heat of their mammal and bird prey. The Fer-de-Lance is the smaller of the two, but it can reach lengths of 7 feet. It is brown with tan bands and blackish blotches, and the tip of its tail is usually yellow.

The Bushmaster can grow to 12 feet, making it the largest poisonous snake in the Americas. It is yellow-tan with dark brown diamond-shaped blotches. Like the Fer-de-Lance, the Bushmaster lives hidden among the fallen leaves of the rain forest floor. Both of these snakes are extremely dangerous.

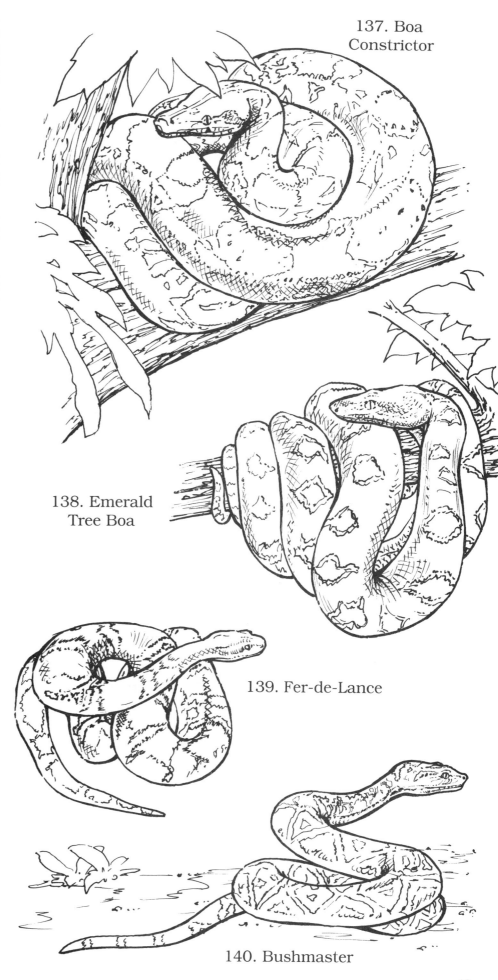

137. Boa Constrictor

138. Emerald Tree Boa

139. Fer-de-Lance

140. Bushmaster

43

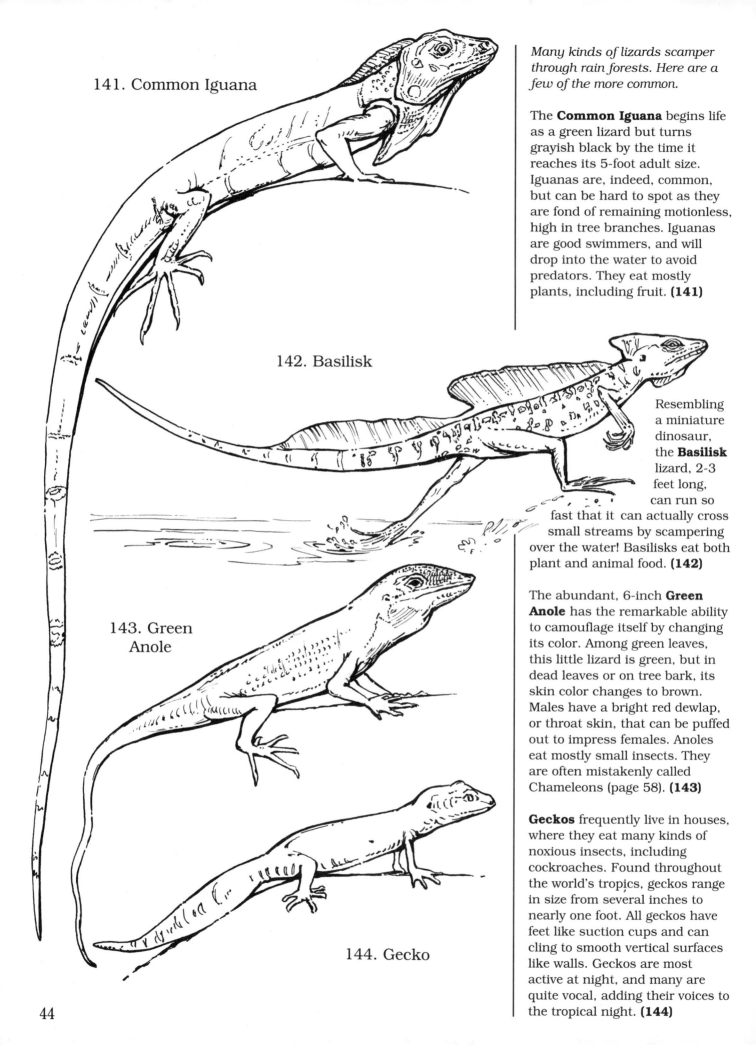

## 141. Common Iguana

## 142. Basilisk

## 143. Green Anole

## 144. Gecko

*Many kinds of lizards scamper through rain forests. Here are a few of the more common.*

The **Common Iguana** begins life as a green lizard but turns grayish black by the time it reaches its 5-foot adult size. Iguanas are, indeed, common, but can be hard to spot as they are fond of remaining motionless, high in tree branches. Iguanas are good swimmers, and will drop into the water to avoid predators. They eat mostly plants, including fruit. **(141)**

Resembling a miniature dinosaur, the **Basilisk** lizard, 2-3 feet long, can run so fast that it can actually cross small streams by scampering over the water! Basilisks eat both plant and animal food. **(142)**

The abundant, 6-inch **Green Anole** has the remarkable ability to camouflage itself by changing its color. Among green leaves, this little lizard is green, but in dead leaves or on tree bark, its skin color changes to brown. Males have a bright red dewlap, or throat skin, that can be puffed out to impress females. Anoles eat mostly small insects. They are often mistakenly called Chameleons (page 58). **(143)**

**Geckos** frequently live in houses, where they eat many kinds of noxious insects, including cockroaches. Found throughout the world's tropics, geckos range in size from several inches to nearly one foot. All geckos have feet like suction cups and can cling to smooth vertical surfaces like walls. Geckos are most active at night, and many are quite vocal, adding their voices to the tropical night. **(144)**

In addition to the colorful dart poison frogs (page 40), many other kinds of frogs and toads inhabit the jungles of Central and South America.

The 3-inch **Gaudy Leaf Frog,** though very colorful, is surprisingly well hidden when tucked among large rain forest leaves. This little tree frog has a bright green upper body, a whitish belly, bluish sides, and orange hands and feet. Its bulging eyes are bright red. **(145)**

The **Giant Marine Toad** is indeed a giant by toad standards — it can get as big as a softball. This bulky, slow-moving dweller of the forest floor is protected from predators by its poisonous skin glands. Its color is uniformly brown. **(146)**

The 5-inch **Marsupial Frog** is named for its unique pouch, located on the lower back of the female. The male helps the female place fertilized eggs inside the pouch, which eventually hatch into tadpoles and develop into miniature frogs before leaving their mother's protective pouch. Marsupial Frogs live in the mountains of Venezuela. **(147)**

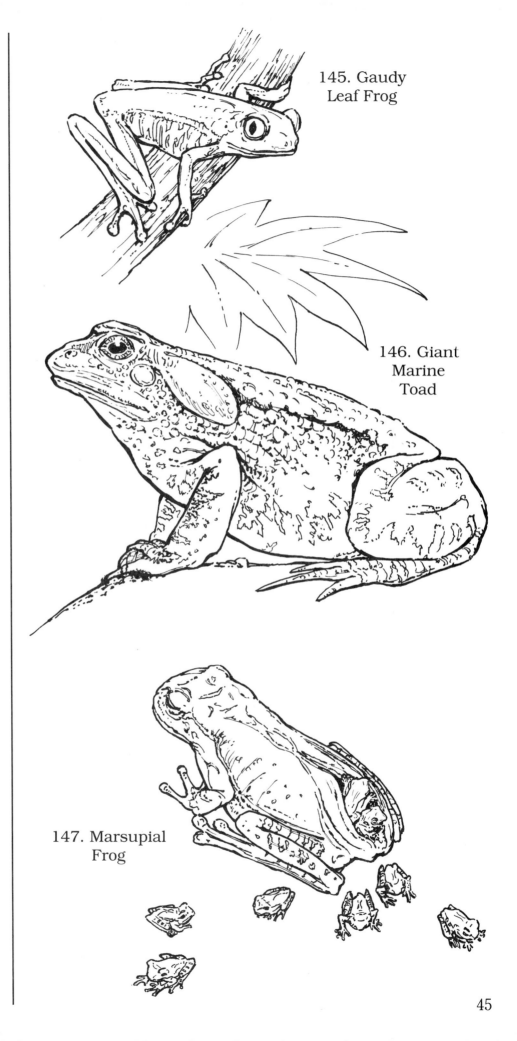

145. Gaudy Leaf Frog

146. Giant Marine Toad

147. Marsupial Frog

154. Hoatzin

## Wildlife of the Amazon River

*More water flows through the Amazon River than any other river in the world. Almost 4000 miles long, the mighty Amazon is home to more kinds of plants and animals than any other river.*

In quiet Amazon pools the immense **Victoria Lily (148)** grows, with conspicous large white flowers and pads fully 6 feet across. Quietly lurking among the lilies might be a golden **Anaconda (149).** The largest of the constrictor snakes, the Anaconda sometimes reaches a length of nearly 30 feet.

Anacondas prey on **Giant Otters (150)** and **Capybaras (151).** The otter reaches a length of 5 feet, not counting its 2-foot-long tail! Capybaras, which resemble giant agoutis, are the largest rodents in the world, reaching weights of 120 pounds.

151. Capybaras

148. Victoria Lily

150. Giant Otter

149. Anaconda

Herds of Capybaras graze like hippopotamuses on aquatic plants. In addition to watching out for Anacondas, Capybaras must be wary of alligatorlike caimans, including the common **Spectacled Caiman (152).**

Birds abound along the Amazon. Overhead soars the huge **Jabirou (153),** a black and white stork with a bulging red neck. Nesting in the dense riverside vegetation, bands of odd **Hoatzins (154),** resembling prehistoric birds, feed entirely on leaves. Baby Hoatzins have claws on their wings. When in danger, they drop into the water and swim safely away, then use their claws to climb back into the trees.

Quietly lurking along the river's edge is the **Sunbittern (155),** a slender bird, mostly reddish with black bars. When it spreads its wings, the Sunbittern reveals bright reddish and black wing patches.

153. Jabirou

155. Sunbittern

152. Spectacled Caiman

## 156. Red Piranha

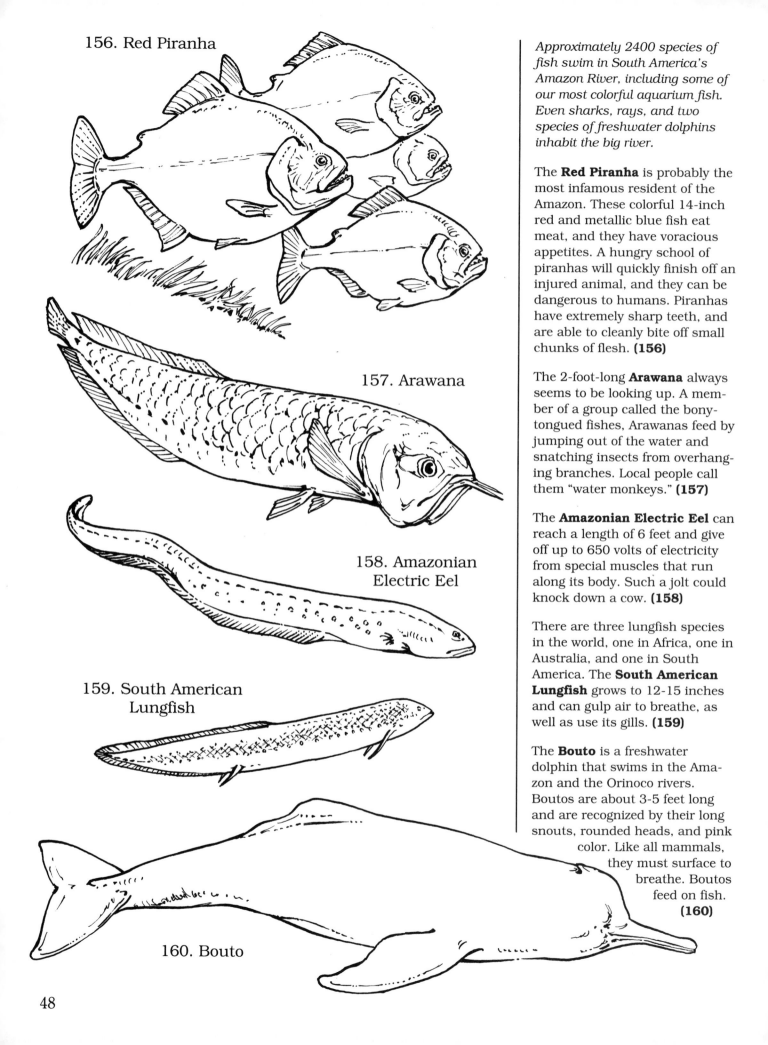

## 157. Arawana

## 158. Amazonian Electric Eel

## 159. South American Lungfish

## 160. Bouto

Approximately 2400 species of fish swim in South America's Amazon River, including some of our most colorful aquarium fish. Even sharks, rays, and two species of freshwater dolphins inhabit the big river.

The **Red Piranha** is probably the most infamous resident of the Amazon. These colorful 14-inch red and metallic blue fish eat meat, and they have voracious appetites. A hungry school of piranhas will quickly finish off an injured animal, and they can be dangerous to humans. Piranhas have extremely sharp teeth, and are able to cleanly bite off small chunks of flesh. **(156)**

The 2-foot-long **Arawana** always seems to be looking up. A member of a group called the bony-tongued fishes, Arawanas feed by jumping out of the water and snatching insects from overhanging branches. Local people call them "water monkeys." **(157)**

The **Amazonian Electric Eel** can reach a length of 6 feet and give off up to 650 volts of electricity from special muscles that run along its body. Such a jolt could knock down a cow. **(158)**

There are three lungfish species in the world, one in Africa, one in Australia, and one in South America. The **South American Lungfish** grows to 12-15 inches and can gulp air to breathe, as well as use its gills. **(159)**

The **Bouto** is a freshwater dolphin that swims in the Amazon and the Orinoco rivers. Boutos are about 3-5 feet long and are recognized by their long snouts, rounded heads, and pink color. Like all mammals, they must surface to breathe. Boutos feed on fish. **(160)**

*Many birds of prey fly above the American rain forests. Some are among the most spectacular in the world.*

The huge **Harpy Eagle** preys on monkeys and sloths. A Harpy Eagle stands 3.5 feet tall, with thick, powerful legs and talons. The largest and one of the rarest of the world's eagles, the Harpy is dark gray with a white belly, black breast band, and gray face. Its head has a ragged crest. **(161)**

The 32-inch **King Vulture** is the world's most colorful vulture, and it is also the largest vulture in the Americas. Its plumage is black and white, but its neck and bill are bright orange. Like all vultures, Kings like to soar high above the forest during the hottest part of the day. **(162)**

A creature of the night, the 19-inch **Spectacled Owl** is named for the white "spectacles" on its otherwise dark brown face. The breast is buffy. Spectacled Owls hunt along forest edges and clearings, snatching prey ranging from insects to birds and mammals. Their deep trembling calls add mystery to the tropical night. **(163)**

The 20-inch **Black-collared Hawk** is found along Amazonian tributary rivers and marshes, where it feeds on fish, frogs, and other aquatic animals. It has a white head, rusty body color, and sharply defined black throat. **(164)**

161. Harpy Eagle

162. King Vulture

163. Spectacled Owl

164. Black-collared Hawk

49

## Tropical Bats

*Bats are remarkable flying mammals of the night. The 40 species that live in the United States all feed on insects captured in mid-air. Of the several hundred species that live in the American tropics, some eat insects, others eat nectar, fruit, fish, frogs, or birds and other bats. Several species feed entirely on blood.*

The **Common Vampire Bat** can scurry mouselike along the ground as it hunts its prey, a sleeping peccary, tapir, or cow. It then makes a tiny cut in the animal's skin and laps up the blood, like a cat lapping milk from a saucer. Vampire bats are warm brown, often with a rusty or silvery tinge to their fur. **(165)**

The reddish **Fishing Bulldog Bat,** with a wingspread of 2 feet, is one of the largest American bats. It uses its sonar (high-pitched squeaks that humans cannot hear) to locate fish breaking the surface of water. The husky bat then flies down and captures the fish, which it grinds up in its big cheek pouches. **(166)**

The odd-looking **Wrinkle-faced Bat** is one of many bat species that feed on fruits. It is light brown with a white shoulder spot and a ladderlike pattern on the underside of its wings. **(167)**

There are many species of **long-tongued bats.** They use their long tongues to reach deep into flowers for nectar. They have no lower front teeth or very small ones, which allows the tongue to push out farther. Most species are small and grayish brown in color. **(168)**

The unmistakable **Ghost Bat** has all-white fur and light tan wings, face, and ears. Ghost Bats feed on insects caught over rivers and lakes or above the canopy. They are sometimes seen fluttering around city lights. **(169)**

165. Common Vampire Bat

166. Fishing Bulldog Bat

167. Wrinkle-faced Bat

168. Long-tongued bat

169. Ghost Bat

## Social Insects

*Without doubt the most abundant animals of the tropical rain forests are the social insects, especially ants and termites. Colonies with immense numbers of workers and soldiers guard a single queen, who is responsible for all of the reproduction of the colony.*

**Leaf Cutter Ants,** also called fungus garden ants, clip leaves from many kinds of plants and carry the leaves to their underground colonies. They use the leaves as fertilizer for their only food source, a unique kind of fungus that these ants grow in "gardens." **(170)**

**Army ants** are carnivorous. They move in large troops over the rain forest floor (see pages 34-35) feeding on insects, spiders, and even small lizards and baby birds. Soldier army ants are much larger than workers and have huge pincerlike jaws. South American army ants are nearly blind but use their sense of smell to follow chemical trails laid down by the workers. African army ants are totally blind. **(171)**

**Termites** feed on wood, digested with the help of tiny one-celled animals that live in their intestines. Many kinds of termites build large, papery nests in trees, with enclosed tunnels running from the nest along the bark. Other termites construct huge, mounded nests in open areas. The queen termite is easily recognized by her immense abdomen. **(172)**

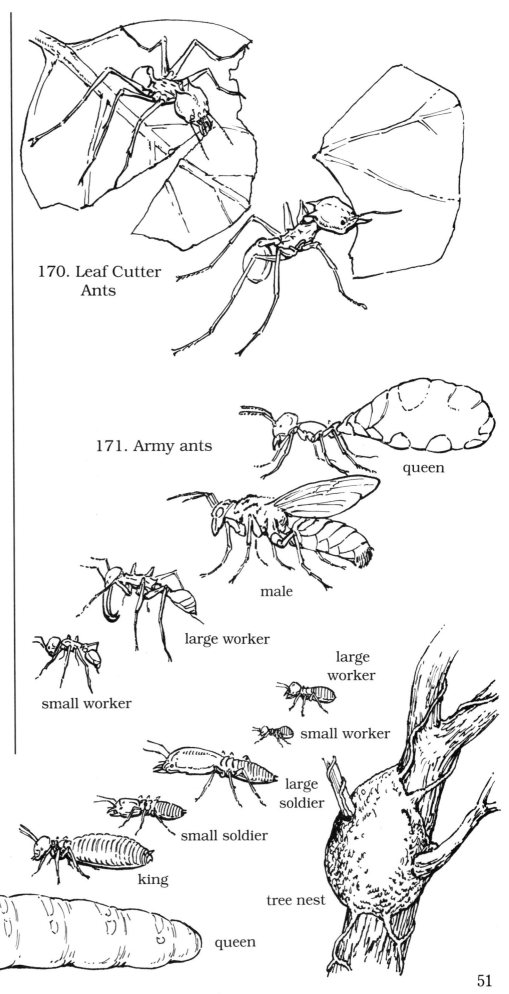

170. Leaf Cutter Ants

171. Army ants

queen

male

large worker

small worker

large worker

small worker

large soldier

small soldier

king

tree nest

172. Termites

queen

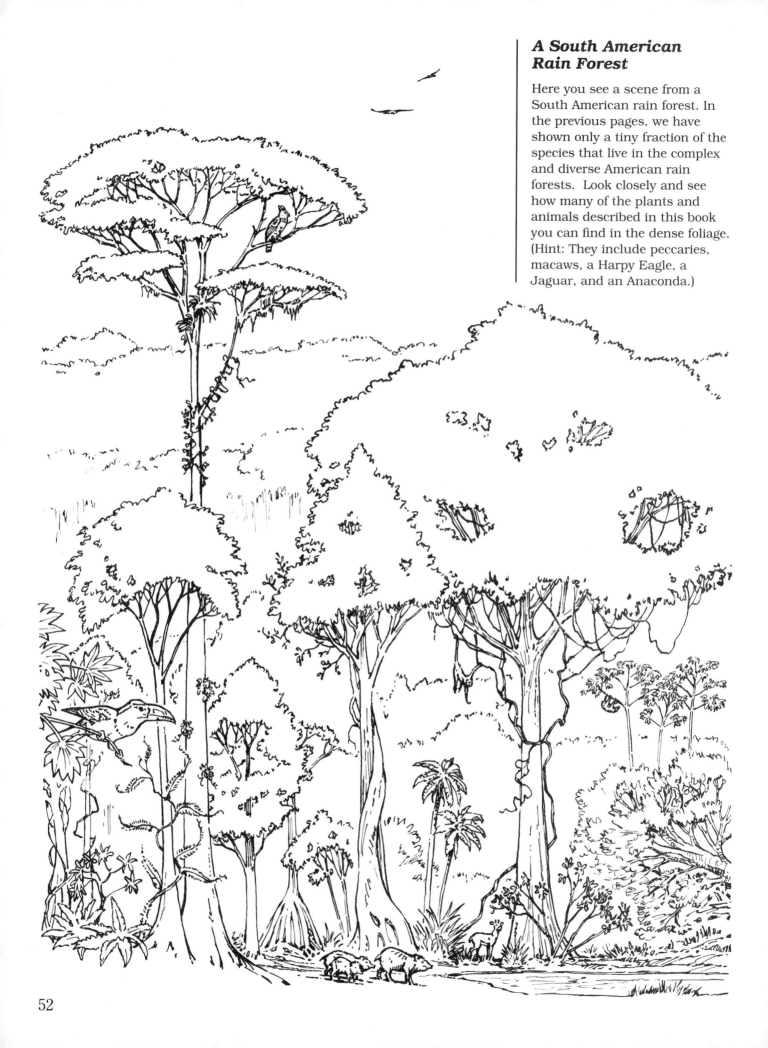

## A South American Rain Forest

Here you see a scene from a South American rain forest. In the previous pages, we have shown only a tiny fraction of the species that live in the complex and diverse American rain forests. Look closely and see how many of the plants and animals described in this book you can find in the dense foliage. (Hint: They include peccaries, macaws, a Harpy Eagle, a Jaguar, and an Anaconda.)

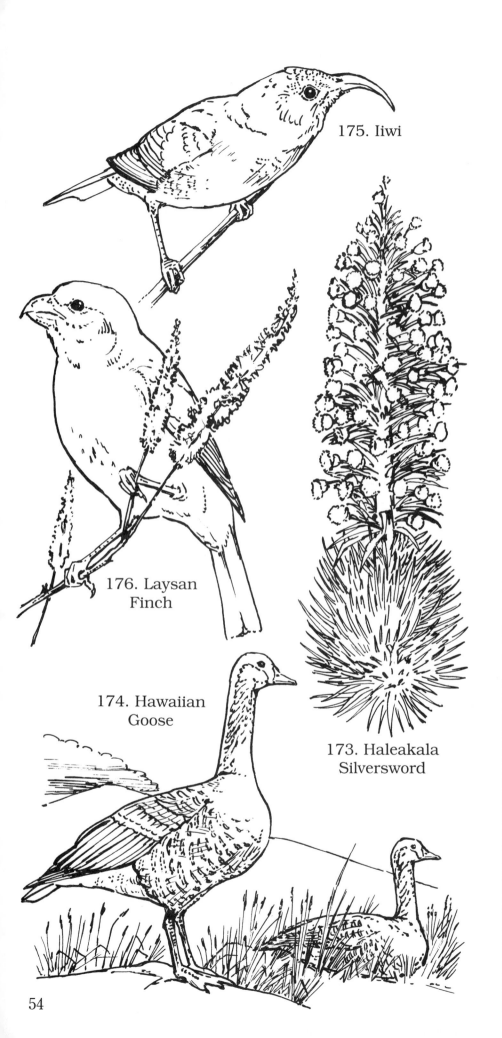

175. Iiwi

176. Laysan Finch

174. Hawaiian Goose

173. Haleakala Silversword

## Rain Forests of Hawaii

*Only one area in the United States can boast true tropical rain forest: the Hawaiian Islands. But much of Hawaii's rain forest treasure has been either destroyed or endangered by introduced animals that have forced out Hawaii's native plants and birds. Some places, like Haleakala on the island of Maui, are protected. They still have the forests and other habitats of these volcanic islands.*

The **Haleakala Silversword,** which grows on the slopes of volcanoes, is not a rain forest plant, but it is representative of the many endangered species found only on Hawaii. Other silversword species do grow in Hawaiian rain forests, but this species is more often seen by visitors. **(173)**

The **Hawaiian Goose,** or Nene, was once almost extinct but has now recovered, thanks to years of successful captive breeding and reintroduction. This medium-sized (25 inches) gray-brown goose can be seen on the slopes of the Mauna Loa volcano and in other locations. **(174)**

Hawaiian honeycreepers are unique Hawaiian birds, found nowhere else in the world. Two species, the **Iiwi (175)** and **Laysan Finch (176),** are illustrated here. Today there are 29 species of honeycreepers, and many of the birds and their habitats are endangered. The Iiwi male is bright red and black, and feeds on nectar obtained with its long curved bill. The Laysan Finch is a yellow, sparrowlike bird that occurs only on the tiny island of Laysan.

## African Rain Forest

*The continent of Africa is best known for vast expanses of savanna, grasslands that host huge herds of antelope, zebra, and other hoofed animals, and their predators, lions, cheetahs, and leopards. However, Africa also has rain and cloud forests. The next three pages illustrate some of the fascinating creatures found in these forests.*

**Gorillas** live both in lowland rain forests and lush, wet mountain forests. Troops of 15 or more females and juveniles are protected by one dominant male. Males are considerably larger than females, weighing up to 600 pounds. Gorillas have black fur and black faces. Older adult males, called "silverbacks," have whitish fur on their backs from shoulders to hips. Gorillas are vegetarians. **(177)**

**Chimpanzees,** which can weigh up to 175 pounds, are smaller than Gorillas, and live in tropical forests and the bordering savanna in central Africa. Chimps eat both plants and animals. They are highly intelligent, and are the only animal besides humans that can make tools: some Chimpanzees will strip the leaves from a stem and use it to fish ants and termites from their mounds. Chimps live in troops of between 30 and 80 animals. Like Gorillas, they are mostly black. **(178)**

The **Mandrill** is recognized by the colorful blue and red skin of its face. A close relative of the baboon, Mandrills live in West African rain forests, where troops of up to 250 feed mostly on plants. Their fur is light brown, and males weigh up to 65 pounds, considerably more than females. Unfortunately, Mandrills are among the most endangered primates. **(179)**

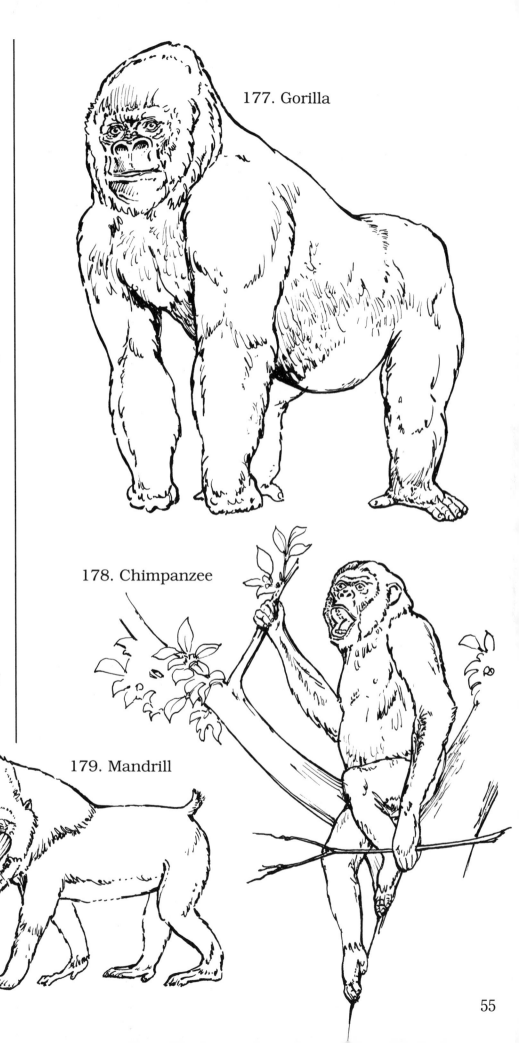

177. Gorilla

178. Chimpanzee

179. Mandrill

55

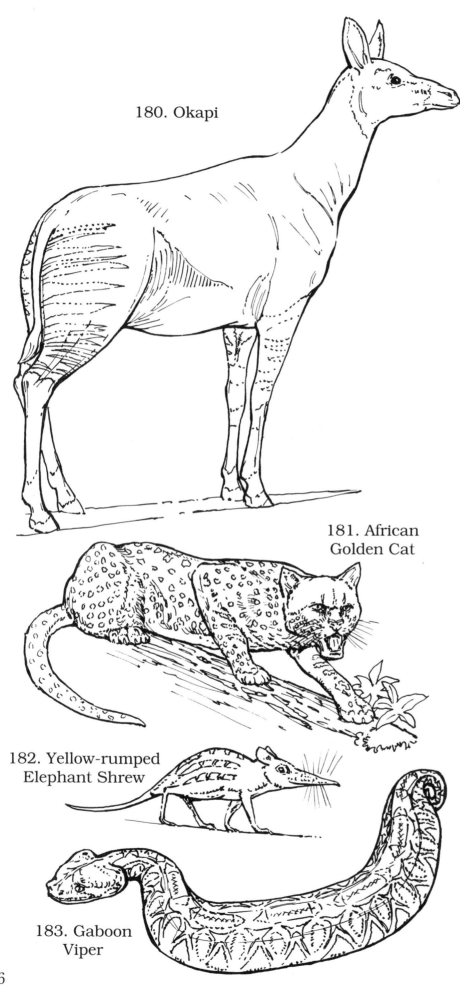

180. Okapi

181. African Golden Cat

182. Yellow-rumped Elephant Shrew

183. Gaboon Viper

The **Okapi** is a kind of small, forest-dwelling version of a Giraffe. Okapis are much smaller than Giraffes, and they don't have a long neck. They are mostly blackish, with a purple sheen. They have a whitish face and hindquarters striped somewhat like a zebra. Okapis live in dense rain forest, where their dark color helps hide them, eating leaves and fruits. They stand about 5 feet tall at the shoulder and weigh up to 550 pounds. **(180)**

The **African Golden Cat** still survives in isolated forests in West and Central Africa, but many of its habitats have been destroyed. Golden Cats are about 30 inches long, with an 18-inch tail. They weigh up to 33 pounds. Their name describes their color, a rich tawny brown with a golden sheen. They hunt a variety of foods, including lizards, rodents, small deer, and birds. A similar species lives in Asia. **(181)**

The 10-inch **Yellow-rumped Elephant Shrew** is named for its yellowish rump and long snout, suggesting an elephant's trunk. With long hind legs and tail, this light brown animal can leap considerable distances. This species is found only in a very small area along the coast of Kenya in East Africa. It feeds on ants, termites, and beetle larvae. **(182)**

The 6-foot-long **Gaboon Viper** is one of the most colorful and deadly snakes of the African rain forest. Ornately patterned in soft brown, gray, and tan diamonds, this snake is well camouflaged among the fallen leaves on the forest floor. The Gaboon Viper has a huge triangular head, which may be as much as 5 inches across. Its poison fangs are 2 inches long. **(183)**

*Africa contains some spectacular rain forest birds. The ones shown here fill mini-habitats from the canopy to the forest floor.*

**Turacos** are slender green birds of the African rain forest and forest edges. They are about 18 inches long, and most of the 18 species have some sort of crest atop the head. The species shown here is metallic green on its head and shoulders, and shiny purple on its wings, back, and tail. It has red markings on its outer wing feathers and around its eyes. Turacos fly rather weakly and feed on fruits in the forest canopy. **(184)**

The **Congo Peafowl** also feeds mostly on fruits that it finds on the forest floor. This colorful pheasant is emerald green on the back and upper wings and metallic blue-black on the rest of its body. It has blue skin on its face, a red throat, and a crest of white and black feathers. This secretive bird of dense forests was discovered in 1936. **(185)**

The **African Pitta** is a chunky, robin-sized, colorful bird that lives on the forest floor, where it searches among leaves for insects, spiders, and small fruits and berries. It has a light green back, red belly, and blue tail. The throat is buffy and the head is black with a white line above the eyes. Pittas are very vocal, but it can be hard to locate the direction of their calls from the forest floor. **(186)**

Up among the canopy branches, flocks of 13-inch **Gray Parrots** search for fruit. Most parrots are green, but this species is uniformly gray, with a white face, black outer wings, and a red tail. Unfortunately for the Gray Parrot, it is much in demand as a pet because it is an excellent mimic and can be taught to "talk." **(187)**

184. Turaco

185. Congo Peafowl

186. African Pitta

187. Gray Parrot

## Madagascar

*The island of Madagascar, off the coast of East Africa, hosts some of the most remarkable rain forest animals and plants. But so much of the forest has been cut down for lumber, many of Madagascar's species are in danger of extinction.*

Among the animals unique to Madagascar are the 20 species of lemurs, a group of primates found nowhere else on Earth. At least 14 lemur species, including a giant one, have recently become extinct. The 15-inch **Ring-tailed Lemur (188)** is gray with a white face and belly and a black and white ringed tail. Its eyes are surrounded with black. Its 20-inch tail is longer than its body. The 30-inch **Indris (189)** is black and white, and it has no tail. Lemurs live in groups, leaping skillfully from tree to tree as they feed on fruits, flowers, and leaves.

Easily overlooked among the foliage is the **Chameleon,** a lizard that may reach almost 2 feet in length. Chameleons have the remarkable ability to change their body coloring to fit their background. When in trees they tend to be green with brown mottling. Chameleons capture insects with their long sticky tongues. They can move their domed eyes in separate directions. **(190)**

The odd **Baobab** tree is unmistakable. This tree of open savannas also grows widely in tropical Africa. Baobabs are an important food and nesting source for many bird and mammal species. **(191)**

188. Ring-tailed Lemur

189. Indris

191. Baobab Tree

190. Chameleon

## India and Asia

*The countries of India, Myanmar, Thailand, Cambodia, and Vietnam contain much of Asia's rain forests. Rates of deforestation are very high in this region.*

Tigers occur from the tropical island of Bali to the cold forests of Siberia and range in weight from about 150 to over 600 pounds. In India, a single **Bengal Tiger** may roam through an area of over 300 square miles, but some places have as many as 14 tigers per square mile (that's a lot of tigers). Orange with black stripes, the tiger is obvious against a plain background but is quite well camouflaged within the shady forest. Tigers feed on both large and small animals. **(192)**

The **Gaur** is sometimes tiger food. This large, black, oxlike hoofed animal may weigh just over a ton, with horns over a yard long. Only males have a shoulder hump. Gaurs live in herds of about 30-40 animals and prefer forested hilly regions near water. **(193)**

The tanklike **Sumatran Rhinoceros** or Asiatic Rhinoceros reaches 10 feet in length and can weigh over 2 tons. It appears to be covered by plates of armor (really just thick skin). Many rhinoceroses are killed because Asiatic peoples believe its horn has medicinal properties. Probably no more than several hundred animals exist in the wild. **(194)**

The **Asiatic Elephant** can be trained to work as a beast of burden. Asiatic Elephants have much smaller ears and a less sloping back than their relatives, the African Elephants. Unlike the African species, the Asiatic Elephant lives in the forest, and deforestation has much reduced its numbers. It feeds on grasses and other vegetation, pulled up with its sensitive, muscular trunk. **(195)**

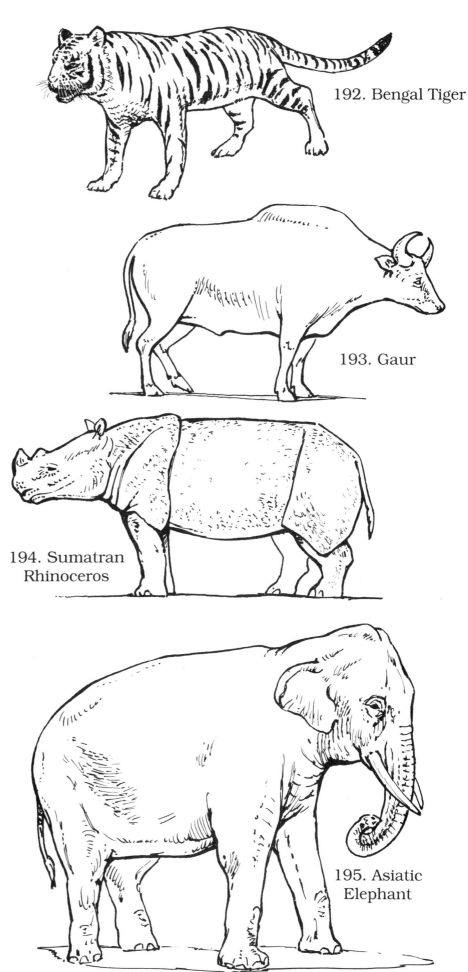

192. Bengal Tiger

193. Gaur

194. Sumatran Rhinoceros

195. Asiatic Elephant

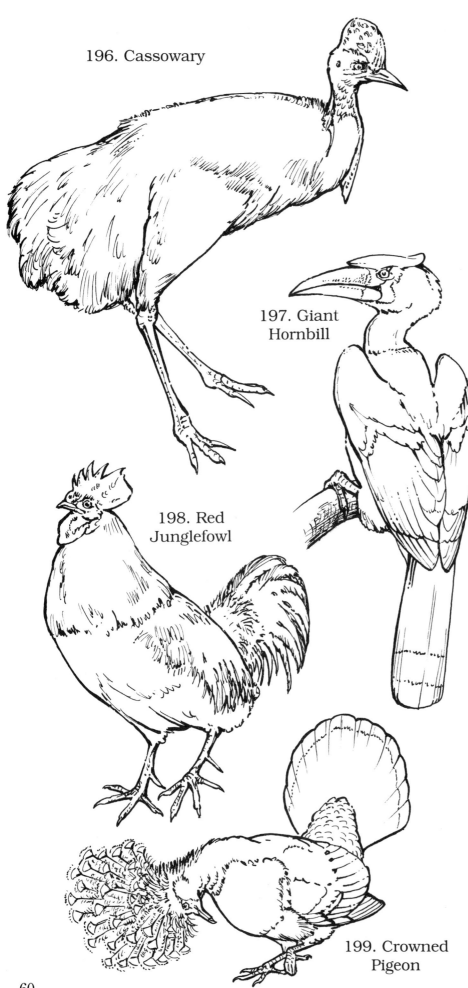

196. Cassowary

197. Giant Hornbill

198. Red Junglefowl

199. Crowned Pigeon

## Asia, Australia, and New Guinea

*Some of the world's most spectacular birds occur in the rain forests of Southeast Asia, New Guinea, and Australia. Here's a sampling from this remarkable collection.*

The flightless **cassowary** can be almost 6 feet tall, but it is surprisingly secretive as it makes its way through shady rain forests of Australia and New Guinea. It is covered by shaggy black feathers, except for the bright blue and red skin on its face and neck. The horny comb atop its head may help the bird pass through dense underbrush or dig up fruits and seeds from the forest litter. **(196)**

Another large rain forest bird is the **Giant Hornbill,** a native of Southeast Asia. This 5-foot-long bird is black and white, with a buffy neck and bill and a buffy "helmet" of light bone atop its head. The bill is long, like a toucan's (page 32). Like a toucan, it feeds mostly on fruits. Females nest in hollow trees, and the male feeds the female and young through a small opening. **(197)**

The **Red Junglefowl** looks like a bantam rooster, and is, indeed, a wild ancestor of our barnyard chickens. A native of Asian forests, the male Red Junglefowl is highly aggressive, using the spurs on its legs to attack other intruding males. Like chickens, Red Junglefowl scratch the forest floor in search of insects and seeds. **(198)**

The **Crowned Pigeon** is just over 2 feet in length, making it the world's largest pigeon. Named for the fan of grayish plumes atop its head, flocks of Crowned Pigeons search New Guinea forests for various fruits. Its body color is rich gray-blue, with violet on the breast and a wide white wing band. The tail also has a white band at the edge. **(199)**

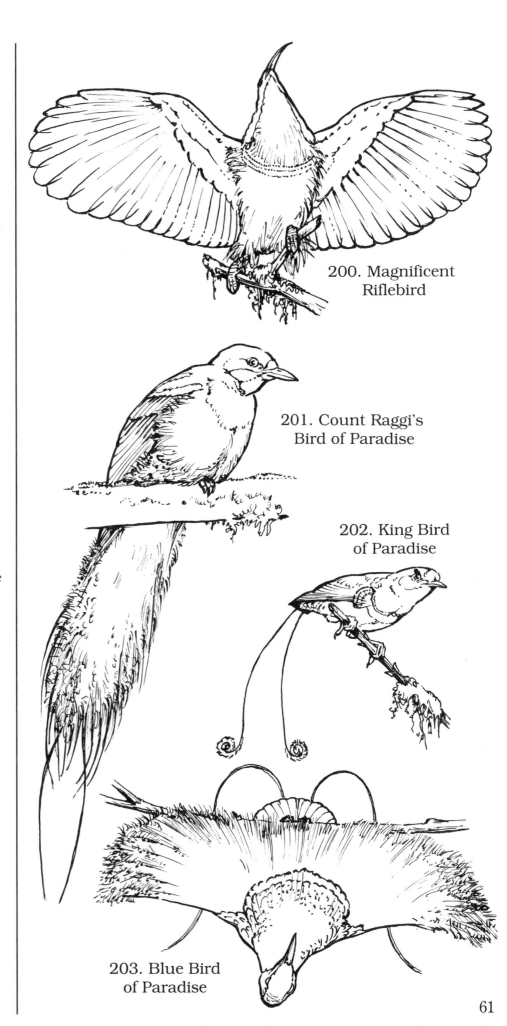

*There are 43 species of birds of paradise in the world, and all live in the tropical forests of New Guinea and Australia. Some qualify as the most colorful birds on Earth. Many of the males have bizarre courtship rituals, in which they show off their spectacular plumage to females.*

The 12-inch **Magnificent Riflebird** male is black with a metallic blue throat and breast, and shiny green atop its head. The female is brown with bars on her breast. Using their long curved bills, riflebirds pluck insects and spiders from the dense vegetation. Males spread their wings wide when courting females. **(200)**

The 13-inch **Count Raggi's Bird of Paradise** is one of the largest and most spectacular of this amazing group. Males have long, delicate red tail plumes, which they spread like a fan when courting. Groups of males gather in the rain forest understory, bowing and spreading their feathers to attract females. Males have a brilliant yellow head and a shiny green throat. Females are brownish and lack the brilliant red plumes of the males. **(201)**

The little 6-inch **King Bird of Paradise** male is bright scarlet above with a white breast and two long, delicate tail plumes with green raquetlike tips. The female, much duller, is mostly brownish gray. Groups of males gather in dense tangles of vines and call females. **(202)**

The 12-inch **Blue Bird of Paradise** male has an uncommonly odd courtship display. He hangs completely upside down from a branch, fanning his delicate blue wing feathers and arching his long tail plumes over him. Any female ought to be impressed by such an effort. **(203)**

200. Magnificent Riflebird

201. Count Raggi's Bird of Paradise

202. King Bird of Paradise

203. Blue Bird of Paradise

## 204. Flying fox

## 205. Flying lemur

## 208. Paradise Tree Snake

## 206. Flying Frog

## 207. Flying dragon

### Animals That "Fly"

*Only insects, birds, and bats can truly fly. The world's largest bats, the flying foxes, live in Old World tropical rain forests, along with several other creatures that have perfected the art of gliding from tree to tree.*

The **flying fox** is a bat with a doglike face. Flying foxes are as large as bats get; some have wingspans of over 5 feet and weigh 2 pounds. There are about 200 species, and they live throughout tropical Africa, Asia, and Australia. Flying foxes eat fruit and are important in spreading the seeds from the fruits. The species from Africa shown here has large brown eyes and reddish brown fur. **(204)**

Colugos, also called **flying lemurs,** live in the rain forests of southeastern Asia. They have a broad skin flap surrounding most of their body, which enables them to "parachute" from tree to tree, much like our familiar flying squirrels. **(205)**

When the green **Flying Frog** jumps from a tree, it spreads its long front and hind toes wide and glides on its webbed feet. This 4-inch-long inhabitant of Thailand, Borneo, and Sumatra can glide up to 40 feet. **(206)**

The **flying dragon** of Southeast Asia is actually a lizard. It can glide up to 20 feet, using flaps of skin supported by its long ribs. Flying dragons are green with black bands. Their skin flaps have orange and black bands. **(207)**

A flying lizard, a flying frog, why not a flying snake? The **Paradise Tree Snake** can escape predators by extending its ribs, flattening itself into a ribbonlike glider. It can leap from a tall tree and glide up to 150 feet. It is brightly colored with bands of red, black, and yellow. **(208)**

## Monkeys and Apes of Asia

*Many remarkable monkeys and apes live in Asian rain forests. Unfortunately, many of them are threatened or endangered by deforestation.*

The unmistakable **Proboscis Monkey** lives in mangrove forests on the coast of Southeast Asia. Males weigh up to 50 pounds and have very large noses (*proboscis* means "nose"). They are mostly gray with a reddish head and back. Though once widely distributed, the species is now confined to parts of Borneo and nearby islands. **(209)**

The **Siamang Gibbon** is a 25-pound black ape that lives in rain forests in parts of Malaysia and Sumatra. It once swung on vines as far north as Myanmar and Thailand, until deforestation drastically reduced its range. Gibbons have long arms, with which they swing from tree to tree. They can scream loudly, much like Howler Monkeys (see page 20). **(210)**

The **Eastern Tarsier** looks like the gnome of the rain forest. This little brown primate, which is only 9 inches long and weighs but 4 ounces, lives only in rain forests of Sulawesi in tropical Asia. It is active mostly at night, as you might guess from its large eyes and big ears. **(211)**

The **Orangutan** searches for fruits, especially figs, in the remaining rain forests of Borneo and Sumatra. Once these shaggy red apes ranged throughout Indochina and Malaysia, but most have disappeared along with their home forests. Male Orangutans are larger than females, and weigh up to 220 pounds. Males have wide, fatty cheek pouches. **(212)**

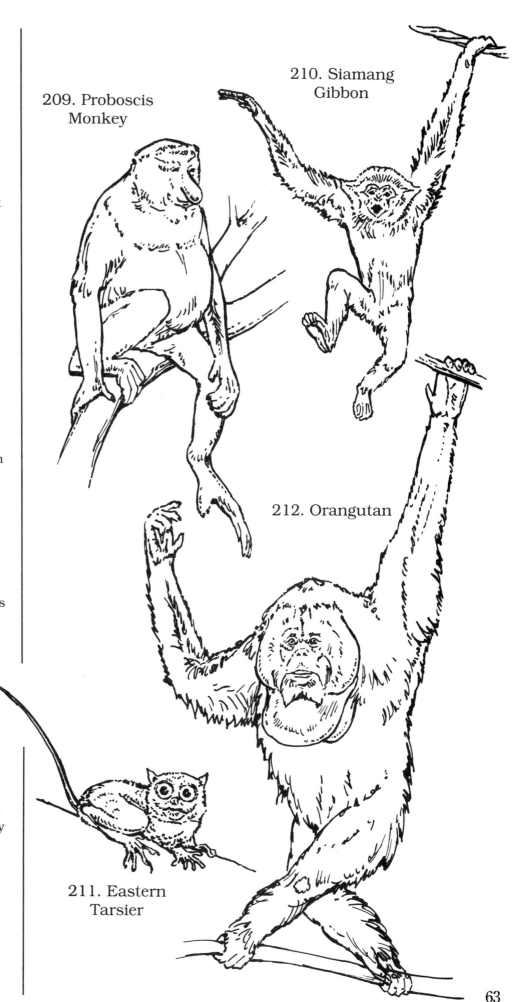

209. Proboscis Monkey

210. Siamang Gibbon

212. Orangutan

211. Eastern Tarsier

## The Future of Our Rain Forests

Already the world has lost over half of its rain forests. People cut them down to get lumber, or burn them to make room for cattle pasture and farmland and to mine minerals. **(213)**

The human population is growing faster in tropical regions than anywhere in the world, and rain forests are often seen as obstacles to improving the life of needy peoples. However, short-term economic gain must be balanced against long-term conservation benefits. Rain forests provide innumerable actual and potential resources for all of the world's people. The amazing number of rain forest plants and animals is a great treasure worth preserving.

It is our hope that this coloring book, which has really only scratched the surface, has helped you to learn more about the magnificent rain forests of our planet. Perhaps you will help to protect them. Visit a rain forest and enjoy!